Thinclads

*A Small-Town 1950s
Track Team
and Then Some*

Richard Van Scotter

Order this book online at www.trafford.com
or email orders@trafford.com

Most Trafford titles are also available at major online book retailers.

Printed in Victoria, BC, Canada.

ISBN: 978-1-4269-0723-4

*Our mission is to efficiently provide the world's finest, most comprehensive book publishing
service, enabling every author to experience success. To find out how to publish your book, your
way, and have it available worldwide, visit us online at www.trafford.com*

Trafford rev. 2/16/2010

 www.trafford.com

North America & international
toll-free: 1 888 232 4444 (USA & Canada)
phone: 250 383 6864 ♦ fax: 812 355 4082

Richard Van Scotter has been a navy ensign, teacher, professor, charter school founder, women's track coach, running circuit racer, curriculum writer, and newspaper columnist.

During his high school years, he worked at a 1950s style drive-in and on a golf course maintenance crew. While in college, he spent summers loading trucks in a lumber yard. More recently, he has written a film script titled *Big Bay Blue* on the early days of the Green Bay Packers. He is the author of several other books on economics, history, education policy, and school culture.

He graduated in 1957 from Elkhorn (Wisconsin) High School, the backdrop for this story. He also has lived in Beloit, Wisconsin; San Francisco, California; Madison, Wisconsin; Park Forest, Illinois; Boulder, Colorado; Grinnell, Iowa; and Boca Raton, Florida. Today, he resides in Colorado Springs, Colorado.

In Memory of Bill Ward

Contents

Preface

In the spring of 2006, *The Elkhorn Independent* newspaper, a small-town Wisconsin weekly, included an article about the local high school track team 50 years earlier. This story recounted the accomplishments of the 880-yard relay team that my brother Roger and I ran on in 1956. I had sent material to Editor Lucas Lauderback, who thoughtfully printed a story on the foursome.

This was an historic team, and one of its members, senior Bill Ward, had died of cancer in October 2003. When Bill's wife Jenny received a copy of the article, she contacted me. They lived in Montoursville, Pennsylvania, where I had visited them a couple years earlier, the first time in decades, during a trip to Hershey about two-hours away.

Jenny Ward learned much about Elkhorn from Bill's boyhood stories and visits to Wisconsin. The story and photo of her husband as a high school boy was nearly overwhelming. She was grateful and commented that the adventures of our team reminded her of the movie *Hoosiers* (1992) starring Gene Hackman and Barbara Hershey. You may remember that the film was about a small-town Indiana high school basketball team in 1954, in which Hackman was the coach and Hershey the school principal.

It was this inspiration that prompted me to write a book that had been stirring within for sometime. The story is titled "Thinclads" a somewhat old-fashion name for track runners, but it is as much about the culture of the area and times, as it is about a high school team and sports. It could be no other way. Growing up in this beautiful southern lakes area of Wisconsin in a vintage small-town with an intriguing history left an indelible impact on my personality and spirit.

My thanks go to Frank Eames who, along with sharing memories, allowed me access to photographs and files from the *Independent*, the weekly newspaper that his family operated for three generations. I also am indebted to Doris Reinke, chair of the Walworth County Historical Society, and my kindergarten teacher in the mid-1940s, who permitted me to use photographs from its archives.

Over the years, I've exchanged ideas with high school teammate Bob Klitzkie, who holds an impressive memory of historical trivia that when viewed collectively offer fond insights. This, Senator Bob does from Guam where he has been a teacher, director of education, attorney, TV show host, and government official since the mid-1960s.

Conversations—by telephone, email, or in person—with Joe Breidenbach, former county clerk and long-time Elkhorn resident; Dick Grimm and Mike Paddock, two athletes instrumental in starting the track program; and teammate, Don Kayser, all helped in the quest for accuracy. Paddock, a former Delta Airline pilot, and Kayser both live in rural country near Elkhorn, while Grimm had been president of a television station and lives in Honolulu, Hawaii.

I also learned significant details from Bill's older sister and younger brother: Mary Ann Pearce operates a farm with her husband near Walworth, Wisconsin, and Jim Ward resides in Albuquerque, New Mexico.

Frank McClellan from nearby Delavan, Wisconsin and classmate at Beloit College provided insider information on the nature of farming and agribusiness in the county. The McClellan family has operated a thriving dairy farm for three generations just outside Delavan en route to Janesville.

The photo of the relay team on the book cover, as well as several others inside, was taken by my oldest brother Bob. At the time, he worked for *The Elkhorn Independent*. When Frank Eames returned from military service in the Navy, he joined the family firm. Bob then became a sports writer for the *Rockford Morning Star*. He is 11-years older than me and a graduate of the Journalism School at Marquette University.

Daughter Shannon Van Scotter, knowing that her dad would overlook some entries, reviewed the manuscript and helped with indexing. Don Van Scotter II, my nephew, provided skilled assistance in preparing photographs.

Finally, Elaine Johnson, former Elkhorn High classmate, read the manuscript, several times, with loving care and provided creative support in designing the cover—front and back.

In 2005, Don, the family's second oldest, wrote a similar book titled *Small-Town Boy* about growing up in Elkhorn during the 1930s and 1940s. He was born nine years before me in 1930. We have two other brothers, and one of them Roger, a year younger than me, is a central character of my story. Growing up in a family of all boys came with some deprivation, and I might have welcomed a sister, but we didn't need more siblings.

In some respects, *Thinclads* is a sequel to *Small-Town Boy*, yet they are distinct books. Don and I are different characters, and this is reflected in our approaches to a similar topic. Let it be said for now that my story comes from the perspective of a cultural critic (meaning to critique not criticize) as well as a young athlete caught up in the pleasures of the time.

A story can take on a life of its own, with the writer going where the narrative leads. My story shifts about three-fourths into it, beginning with *Life after High School.* Here, I start to use the first person pronoun. Until then I am just a character and participant referred to in the third person. The reader should be warned that in the latter part of the book, I liberally offer social commentary with a retrospective view on society. Nevertheless, I trust you will find that this personal perspective relates to and never veers from the major themes—community, character, and culture.

No one should think this book irreverent; it is written from the heart and soul as well as the mind. I will understand, however, if some feel it lacks the requisite modesty. While I write this story with pride, it is a humbling experience to reflect on one's past complete with its blemishes and supporting cast.

I trust you will find the reading thought-provoking and even a little amusing.

Richard Van Scotter
Colorado Springs, Colorado

1.   Elkhorn High School circa 1950

1 **An American Original**

A page of history is worth a volume of logic.
Oliver Wendell Holmes

Track and field came late to the Southern Lakes Conference in southeast Wisconsin. It wasn't until 1954 that conference schools officially recognized the world's most popular sport and centerpiece of the Olympic Games. Until then male athletes at Elkhorn High School had to select between baseball and tennis in the spring.

Wisconsin high school track competition dates to the late 1800s, and the state has the distinction of conducting the nation's first official state track championship in May of 1895 at the University of Wisconsin in Madison. The first state track champion crowned under WIAA (Wisconsin Interscholastic Athletic Association) rules was Milwaukee West in 1897, although Milwaukee East is recognized as the first winner in 1895.

Milwaukee public high schools dominated state track finals over the first four decades of the 1900s, running off a string of championships from 1914 to 1926. They repeated the feat all but two years from 1928 to 1941. Madison High put together a mini-string from 1909 to 1911, while Kenosha interrupted the Cream City's reign in 1927 as did Green Bay West (1934) and Appleton (1937) during the following decade.

The supremacy is no surprise because Milwaukee was a national leader in developing the American comprehensive high school in the early 1900s, a time when nationwide less than 15 percent of 14–to–17 year olds were in school. The industrial revolution was building a "head of steam" in the United States, and secondary education was becoming increasingly critical for citizenship and the U.S. economy. Besides, communities now had to figure out what to do with the growing number of boys and girls who no longer had farm work and other jobs to do. The cornerstone schools of this "beer capital" were Milwaukee East, West, North, South, Washington, and Bay View high schools.

From 1895 to 1919, competition followed a one-class format where schools of all sizes competed together. Nevertheless, most early track teams represented larger high schools in cities such as Wausau, Stevens Point, Oshkosh, La Crosse, Racine, Beloit, and Waukesha, along with Milwaukee and Madison. The state meet went to two classes from 1920 to 1926; thereafter, Wisconsin conducted a three-class interscholastic track and field system into the twenty-first century.

Elkhorn tucked away near the Illinois border in Walworth County was not one that sponsored interscholastic track and field programs. In fact, no high school in the county had "thinclad" teams. The term seems quaint today but was a popular label in the early to mid-1900s. During the 1920s, the county sponsored area-wide meets that drew youngsters from across its townships, but the small high schools didn't venture to Madison's Camp Randall Stadium on the university campus to test their talents against the big-city boys at the annual state competition.

♪

Walworth country exhibits the traditional dimensions of territories surveyed with the Land Ordinance of 1785, also known as a Northwest Territory. Five states came to occupy the then northwest landscape, and Wisconsin was the last to gain statehood in 1848. The others were Ohio (1803), Indiana (1816), Illinois (1818), and Michigan (1837). This historic 1785 land measure established a plan for dividing counties, where feasible, into townships of 36 square miles—six miles on a side. Walworth County rests west of and adjacent to Racine and Kenosha counties in the southeastern region of the state with its southern boundary resting on the Illinois border. To the west is Rock County whose two major cities—Beloit and Janesville—are considerably larger than any in Walworth County.

The county assumed the classic configuration of 16 townships, in a symmetric four-by-four square with Elkhorn resting squarely in the middle among four townships—Sugar Creek, Lafayette, Delavan, and Geneva. This reflects Thomas Jefferson's vision of a rational landscape, easy to navigate, in an aesthetically pleasing grid. The population of the county today is just over 100,000 with its four largest cities—Whitewater, Delavan, Lake Geneva, and Elkhorn—having around 10,000 residents each. Its other municipalities, including Walworth, Darien, Sharon, Williams Bay, East Troy, Genoa City, and Fontana on Geneva Lake, are villages.

Elkhorn configures to the Jeffersonian ideal with streets bearing the names of presidents Washington, Lincoln, Jackson, Adams, Jefferson, and Van Buren. Fanning from the court house square are Broad, Church and Court. The thoroughfares—Wisconsin, Walworth, and Geneva—recognize the state, county and township respectively.

The state's first 4-H club was founded on a farm in nearby Linn Township just five months after Congress passed the Smith-Lever Act in May 1914. This legislation established the Cooperative Agency Service, bringing together federal, state, and local governments and setting up County Extension Services to assist farmers.

Given its central location, Elkhorn was the natural choice for a county seat. With county dimensions 24 miles on each side, the roundtrip from Whitewater in the northwest corner, to conduct business in Elkhorn, was a day's journey on horseback in 1850.

From another perspective, Elkhorn is located at the crossroads of Chicago (80 miles to the southeast), Milwaukee (45 miles to the northeast), and Madison (60 miles to the northwest). In the 1950s, travelers made their way along U.S. Route 12 from Chicago to Madison and possibly beyond to Eau Claire and the Twin Cities. In so doing, they would come through Elkhorn just as would those on U.S. Route 15 out of Milwaukee to Beloit, which rests on the Illinois border.

In 1955, Elkhorn was still a small community of about 3,500 residents, nestled among dairy and cattle farms. Its main industry centered on agriculture, country government, and the manufacture of band instruments.

The city was settled in the 1830s by Colonel Samuel Phoenix, who as the story goes, spotted a rack of Elk antlers in a tree near where a few settlers had come and called the site "Elk Horn." The locale had 14 residents in 1837 and by 1846 had grown to 539, when the first town meeting was held. The area's beauty prompted Milwaukee speculators Daniel Bradley, his brother Milo, and LeGrand Rockwell to acquire land and create a village in the middle of the county. Not long after, it was incorporated as a city and declared the county seat in 1851. That same year the county fair was first held in Elkhorn, and over time it grew into one of the outstanding expositions across the Badger State and nation. Other villages nearby also were gaining a footing in the fertile soil and around the beautiful lakes left by the migration of glaciers that had traversed the area thousands of years earlier.

Subsequently, early industry and major sources of employment in the town were based on agriculture, particularly dairy farming. This region of the heartland harvested cash crops, including corn, oats, hay, barley, and wheat as well as sweet corn, peas, and beans for canning. The milk plant and cannery on the south end of the city, and the farm cooperative downtown reflected its rural base. During World War II, the cannery and dairy were busy producing food for the troops as well as civilian population. And the plants offered employment for high school students and others, who worked alongside German prisoners of war. From its beginning, the area attracted immigrants from central Europe, particularly Germany, Great Britain, and Scandinavia.

One of the county track and field competitors in the early 1920s was high jumper Perry MaGill whose father, Fred, and uncle, Willis, operated a plumbing business in Elkhorn. The brothers also were original members of the well-known Elkhorn Holton band. Frank Holton, a manufacturer of cornets, trombones, French horns, and other brass instruments, moved his company from Chicago to Elkhorn in 1918. Residents celebrated with a parade through town, and the Holton factory became the city's main manufacturer. In 1939, Tony Getzen, plant supervisor at Holton's, left to start his own band instrument firm in a converted barn on the south side of town. Soon he was joined by sons, Robert, Donald, and William. Elkhorn became known as a music town and today includes a symbol of a horn for the letter "O" in its name on signs and the water tower.

The "music town" also lays claim to the home of Joseph Philbrick Webster, a famous 19th century composer and author of such popular Civil War songs as "Lorena" composed in 1857, the year he moved to Elkhorn, and the "Sweet Bye and Bye" written during the war. Webster resided in his home, which is now a museum, until his death in 1875. The Webster House also serves as the Walworth County Historical Society.

In 1926, a few years after Holton's arrival, a band shell was built on the north end of the two-block long court house square, where it remained for years until relocated to a new city park on the edge of town. With its special background for performers, the venue had wonderful acoustics. City folks crowded the park on summer evenings to converse, enjoy popcorn, and hear the Elkhorn band perform. Rarely a holiday passed without the Drum and Bugle Corp leading a parade through the village. Out front was Fred Platts astride his bay mare "Lady," known as the dancing horse, as she pranced to the music and delight of onlookers.

2 And Sports Town

A man is not old until regrets take the place of dreams.
Actor John Barrymore

County-wide track and field contests in the 1920s were held at the "College Field" in Williams Bay. Young MaGill, who went on to Beloit College, where he set the high jump record at 5'9", was a county standout. Churning up cinders and jumping into saw dust pits was a club sport in those days. Football in the fall and basketball during those long Wisconsin winters were the games that Elkhorn boys thrived on each school year. The mid-1940s became a banner time at Elkhorn High School for the two sports.

The original gymnasium, built in 1906, was a small, bandbox facility where any youngster with a decent stroke could make a set shot from center court. Players dribbled on to the basketball court from the basement level, while fans entered from the main floor on to a balcony that circled the court about 10 feet overhead. They congregated in the balcony for a view of the game floor, and players shooting from the corners discovered that the trajectory of the ball could be interrupted by the balcony overhang. Players dealt with these conditions until 1938 when a new high school was built adjacent to the old building on North Jackson Street.

Thanks to the Roosevelt Administration, the school was part of the federal government's Works Project Administration (WPA) during the Great Depression to revive the U.S. economy. About this time, the WPA also was building a post office at the corner of Walworth and Washington Streets. With other national projects, including The Cow Palace in San Francisco, LaGuardia Airport in New York, and Chicago's Lake Shore Drive Outer Bridge, the new EHS was transforming the physical face of America. It was a beautiful, state-of-the-art structure designed to accommodate 300 students during the late 1930s and war years of the forties. Its art deco style also was popular with American hotels, public buildings, and movie theaters of the era. The show piece of the school was the then spacious gymnasium located on its northeast corner. Because it was one of the most appealing athletic facilities in the area, with a seating capacity of about a 1000, the Elkhorn Kinne Gym hosted several regional basketball tournaments during the 1940s.

The fascination of economics is in being both logical and counterintuitive. Elkhorn benefited from this paradox in the waning years of the Great Depression. It was only *logical* for individuals and households to reduce spending at the time. In fact, they had no other choice when unemployed or underemployed. Yet, what's true for the individual is not necessarily true for people collectively. When all cut back, it is detrimental to the economy, as aggregate demand sharply declines.

Enter the *counterintuitive* part where government injects a fiscal stimulus, such as the WPA and other projects of the 1930s and The Reinvestment and Recovery Act in 2009. People are inclined to prescribe what's good for the individual to government. This, however, would be harmful. If government doesn't intervene to rejuvenate spending and stimulate the economy, the recession will deepen. And yes, this creates budget deficits—which are a bad thing in normal times but actually a good thing when the economy slumps.

Acting together, as a team, "We the People" can accomplish what is imprudent and unrealistic alone.

In the cold, snowy winter of 1945-46, Elkhorn High basketball fans were in for a treat. The home team anchored by 6'7" center Don "Tiny" Millard breezed through conference play undefeated and ended the regular season 15 and 1; their only loss coming in an early upset to non-conference foe Milton Union. The Elks fielded one of the area's taller teams that year with senior Bill Seymour and junior Bob Sorenson manning the front line along with Millard. By current standards the two forwards might not be considered tall. Yet, during the harsh winter of '46, when the snow measured 6 feet high along the sidewalks lining Washington Street, Bill Seymour's head could be seen above the drifts.

The then Southern State Conference included five teams: Delavan Comets, Whitewater Whippets, Lake Geneva Resorters, and Burlington Demons in addition to Elkhorn. In 1946, Lake Geneva was the largest school with 350 students, while Elkhorn had 256.

As host of the regional tournament that March, the "Elks five" waltzed through with victories over Burlington, Beloit (a perennial power in the elite Big Eight Conference), and Oconomowoc. After winning the opening game of the sectional tournament at Nathan Hale High in West Allis over Wilmot 40 to 24, and sporting a 17–game winning streak, they fell to Racine Park, another Big Eight school, by a lopsided score 53 to 26. With it, Elkhorn's dream of a first trip to Madison and state tournament vanished. Wisconsin Interscholastic basketball at the time, unlike track and field, was a one-division enterprise, and Elkhorn, as with other conference schools, had to get past Big Eight and suburban Milwaukee teams in order to make it to "state." This, no Elks squad did from 1916 until 1972 when prep basketball went to two classes.

What a delight if the Elks had made it to the state tournament in 1946 and gone up against Reedsville, the eventual winner, an even smaller school with just 92 students in a town of under 800 people. In winning the title, Reedsville put away Racine Park, Wisconsin Rapids, and Eau Claire—all much larger schools.

While the Elkhorn basketball team that season benefited from senior leadership, the "football eleven" had capable undergraduates at all positions. It was a confident Elkhorn squad that prepared for the fall 1946 football season in a newly formed 8-team SWANI Conference. The SWANI, an acronym for Southern Wisconsin and Northern Illinois, included three schools across the state line: Harvard, Marengo, and McHenry. Showing off new uniforms (white jerseys, purple lettering, and purple pants with gold stripes down the back), the aggressive Elks rushed through the season undefeated—shutting out five opponents while outscoring all by the margin of 146 to 26. With no football playoffs during this era, the Elks didn't know how they might have fared on a larger stage. This also was Elkhorn's season of "Original Friday Night Lights," when for the first time they could play in the evening and draw larger crowds. The '46 team included sons of prominent families bearing such names as Jones, Morrissey, Eames, Sorenson, Jacobsen, Reed, Cusack, Dunbar, Hanny, Heusser, Skoine, and Schmidt.

The SWANI Conference was short-lived, spanning seven years from 1946 to 1953, after which Harvard and Marengo migrated to the Shark Conference in Illinois and McHenry to the North Suburban. Beginning with the 1953–54 school year, East Troy, Mukwonago, and Wilmot joined the original five schools in a newly formed Southern Lakes Conference. Since its inception,

Elkhorn has been a perennial member over the league's 50–plus year history. Others would depart and return and some depart again as enrollments changed and new schools were born, but only Elkhorn and Delavan remained as conference anchors over the years.

After that 1946 season, the Elks fell into a "pigskin slumber" and didn't capture a conference football title until 30 years later, when they again went undefeated. The climate was different in basketball. The Elks prided themselves as a "basketball school" also winning conference titles in '44–'45, '50–'51, '51–'52, '57–'58, '58–'59, and '61–'62. Yet, in none of those years, did they make it out of the regional tournament. This they would accomplish in '60–'61, a non-title year, where they upset conference champ Lake Geneva (now Badger High) and Beloit Memorial in the regional final by a 77–74 score.

The end of the line that season came in the sectionals when the "purple and gold" fell to Madison West, another Big Eight conference power. Elkhorn eventually captured back–to–back Wisconsin state basketball titles in the late 1970s, but by then they played in a three-classification system, competing among mid-size, Class B schools, now referred to as Division II. With this, the road to Madison was less challenging.

The seeds of Elkhorn's success in sports are sowed on its open lawns and fields where kids make up football contests, on sandlots where baseball diamonds are created, and especially in the driveways of homes where basketball hoops hang over garage doors. Throughout the cold Wisconsin winters, it was commonplace for Elkhorn youngsters to play basketball outdoors until fingers became numb and snow too high for anything but climbing drifts and dunking the ball. Without a recreational center in town, the primary indoor opportunity of grade school boys to sharpen their court skills were the Friendly Indians (4th–6th grade) and Pioneers (7th–8th grade) competition held Saturday's during basketball season in the 1906 gym. Occasionally, teams would make the 28-mile trip to the YMCA in Janesville for basketball contests and swimming.

An unjust and unequal fact of life in those days was that interscholastic sports were restricted to boys, while high-school-age girls only had an intra-school GAA (Girls' Athletic Association). There was little competition between towns for young women. One exception to the national trend was Iowa high school basketball, where the sport was practiced with such vigor that the girls' games and tournament play often outdrew the boys'. Thanks to women's awareness movements and liberation, this would change dramatically in the 1970s.

The average family in the 1950s numbered two parents and about 3.5 children with the fertility rate reaching 3.8 in 1957, the "baby boom" peak. It was not unusual, particularly for rural families, to have five or more children. By age 10, farm girls were learning to cook, tending to household chores, and milking cows, while boys were caring for livestock, helping plow fields, and baling hay. Given the demographics, nearly every town has its "band of brothers" that provided talent to the athletic teams. Elkhorn was no exception.

In the early 1930s, Jim (class of '31) and Lawrence ('33) Hutton followed by the Thompson brothers— Lloyd ('36) and Glenn ('37) stood out. In the 1940s, Bill ('46) and Bob ('47) Morrissey starred in football, basketball, and baseball. The Breidenbachs—Joe ('40), Don ('45), and Gary ('59) spanned 19 years, while Ted ('45) and Hilbert "Bud" Heusser ('48) were bulwarks on the football and basketball teams that stretched from 1943 to 1948. They were followed by the Joneses—Trevor ('44), Don ('47) and Phil ('49). Stan Wilson ('41) was several years older than his twin brothers, Don and Ron ('50) who, though small in stature, added zip on the football field as halfbacks from 1947 through 1949.

In the fifties came Jim ('55) and Jon ('58) Platts, all-conference performers on the playing field, hard court, and baseball diamond. Don ('55) and Ralph ('56) Morello were transplants from the Chicago area. About that same time, the Riese brothers—Bill ('57), Don ('60), and Terry ('62) played key roles on the football, track, and baseball squads. Then there were the Wuttkes: Don ('47) starred as a halfback and defensive back on the undefeated 1946 team; Jim ('58) was all-conference in 1957, as an offensive guard and linebacker; and John ('62) a two-way, all-conference lineman. The Van Scotter brothers made their mark in three decades: first Bob ('46) and Don ('48) followed by Richard ('57), Roger ('58), and Alan ('62).

Bob earned football honors as a halfback and was catcher on the baseball team. All of the younger "Van boys" excelled in four sports, setting school records, earning state titles, and winning conference rushing, scoring, and batting crowns. Each was recipient of the American Legion Medal awarded to the top senior class athlete in their respective years. The family of Henry and Helen Van Scotter has been the only three-time winner of this honor in its long history. Of course, it took five attempts. Given other trends, however, the family was fortunate that one was not a dim-wit—or maybe it wasn't officially acknowledged.

The Legion medal originated in Elkhorn in 1922. The first to receive the award was Wilford Opitz, a county track champion. Legion Post commander, Will A. Foster, suggested the idea of honoring a top high school athlete at the state convention, and other towns throughout Wisconsin followed Elkhorn's lead. In time, the award spread to cities across the country.

Roger and Richard (Dick) with Don also were selected to represent Elkhorn at Badger Boys State on the campus of Ripon College.

3 **Conservative and Provincial**

*My definition of a free society is a society where it is
safe to be unpopular.*
Adlai Stevenson

Walworth County is rural Midwest Republican
country. This is the land of independent farmers
and small business owners who want government
small and the freedom to pursue their "enlightened"
self interest. In this respect, many also are Jeffersonian
republicans (with a small "r"). Any inequality that results
is justified and will be sufficiently taken care of through
local benevolence. Yet, the people here come together in
community activities, conduct grand patriotic parades
on national holidays, and hold a classic county fair
every summer over Labor Day weekend.

While many areas of the nation are moving away from
such pastoral celebrations, the county fair in Elkhorn,
Wisconsin grows each decade. Attendance for the six-day
event in recent years has been about 175,000—far more
than the number of residents in the county. Virtually,
everybody attends and many participate: children show
their prize animals, adults work exhibit halls, young

women race horses while men showcase tractors and trucks, auctioneers sell their animals, and all seem to enjoy the carnival rides, grandstand entertainment, and comfort food.

The county is an anomaly against the long history of progressive politics from its state capitol in Madison and tradition of socialist mayors in Milwaukee. To its east and along Lake Michigan shores lay Racine and Kenosha counties, defined by their manufacturing industries, ethnic populations, and heavily Democratic constituents, that stand in contrast to the WASP (white, Anglo-Saxon Protestant), small-town, rural culture of Walworth County. Much the same can be said for Rock County on its Western border where its major cities, Beloit and Janesville, have an industrial base and more diverse populations.

Walworth County citizens consistently support the Republican candidate for political offices, even when the politician abandons conservative principals. People here are inclined to trust a GOP candidate even if it requires believing the rhetoric and ignoring the behavior. In 1952, Elkhorn's 8th grade social studies class, of which 13-year-old Dick Van was a member, conducted a mock Presidential election. Republican Dwight Eisenhower was a near unanimous winner—17 votes to one over Democrat Adlai Stevenson. The lone dissenter lived outside the city limits and was the son of an industrial worker employed in a neighboring city. Despite increasing the size of government; running up large, non-wartime, budget deficits; and leading the nation down the "path of profligacy," citizens of the county overlooked this neglect of conservative and republican principles and eagerly supported Ronald Reagan in the 1980s. The "Gipper" was one of theirs, having grown up 90-minutes away in Dixon, Illinois. These resourceful, industrious people also supported ne'er-do-well George W. Bush—twice.

This rural county also is Protestant country. The courthouse square in Elkhorn is surrounded by churches, including St. Patrick's Catholic. A sprinkling of Jewish and other believers also are among the local citizenry, but one would have to look some to find anyone who professed to being an atheist, agnostic, or secular humanist. Despite a rich history in America, Quakers do not have a meeting house in the community, and a small Unitarian-Universalist congregation would come much later.

Ethnic diversity and racial tolerance have not been signature characteristics of this traditional town. This, however, is changing. During the 1950s when civil rights was stirring the conscience of a nation and entering the courts, it met with indifference in Elkhorn. Unlike the Deep South, the racism generally was implicit and understated. Yet, it was not uncommon to hear, or at least feel, the "N-word" conveyed by a student in school or anyone when a car of "negroes" drove through town, making their way from Chicago to places north along busy Highway 12.

Rumor has it that until the 1940s blacks could not remain overnight in Elkhorn. Although no evidence of a city-wide ordinance has been found to exist, this belief was pervasive and effective—northern-style "Jim Crow." For whatever reason, Jack Dale, the African-American barber shop shoeshine man, lived in nearby Delavan. Like most prejudice and bigotry, this was an expression of fear couched in an attitude of racial superiority. Such is not the republicanism of Abraham Lincoln but rather of the "Know-Nothing" Party founded in 1849 with a platform based on the rejection of immigrants, particularly Irish, Catholics, and generally anyone who did not fit the white, Protestant profile. Yes, the "Know-Nothings" actually existed, officially the American Party. It dissolved by 1860, but the spirit lives on.

In a small but significant way, the movement from racism in middle-America towards more equality for minorities is part of a larger progressive shift in the nation's history. A tacit prejudice still exists, but the target has changed to Hispanics, who ironically fill critical job needs in agriculture and service industries. Most not only bring a strong work ethic but also maintain a "focus on the family."

By the 1950s, the town's new complexion announced a gradual shift in political attitude. After World War II, Elkhorn and neighboring areas experienced a migration of inhabitants largely from the Chicago area. Chicagoans, familiar with the peaceful and beautiful surroundings of the Wisconsin landscape with its lakes, rolling hills, and small villages, packed their belongings and moved to Wisconsin. Walworth County was the first stop over the border, and many Illinois transplants raised families in the safe, small-town environment and made a living as farmers, doctors, lawyers, resort owners, restaurateurs, and other vocations.

Two escapees from Chicago, of Italian decent, were Sperino and Mary Maile. They settled in Elkhorn, built a home, started a restaurant, and shortly thereafter, Sperino ran for sheriff—as a Democrat. As neighbor Helen Van Scotter announced not long after Sperino's arrival, "He's both a Wop and Democrat!" But youngsters in the village appreciated the new arrivals—as Morello, Colombe, Giovannoni, Kieraldo, Vlad, Valerio, and Olivas introduced their customs, style, and talents and in so doing contributed a slice of diversity to the school culture.

An amusing aspect of small-town culture and politics could be found in barber shops, corner gas stations, and bars where the "town criers" spread their "wisdom." The observant grade school boy came to realize the educational value of these "wind bags," and how this was a building block to critical thinking—otherwise known as "crap-detecting." In time, it would prove handy in deciphering the "balderdash" spewed forth on AM Talk radio.

Elkhorn was changing, and this modification would become substantial. Walworth County tilted toward Presidential candidate John McCain in 2008, in this decidedly "blue state," but Elkhorn bucked the historic trend when a majority of voters "pulled the lever" for Barack Obama. The last election in which Elkhorn citizens supported a Democratic candidate was for Franklin Delano Roosevelt deep into the Great Depression. These people have a canny intelligence; when capitalism falters, many turn to rational economic policies. It could be said that they are even "closet Keynesians."

Not only was Chicago influencing this provincial town, but urban Milwaukee transplants were moving out, building homes in subdivisions, and threatening to turn Elkhorn into an "exurb," as it had with nearby Mukwonago (for Milwaukee) and McHenry (for Chicago). With this "population explosion," largely since 1990, the town of 2,500 denizens in 1940 now approached 10,000.

Many newcomers are Democrats, or at least Independents, who feel that the GOP needed to retool and reboot. Even long-time residents of the county, like many in the Northeast and Midwest, lament that the party has drifted from its traditional republicanism and been captured by a narrow Southern, anti-immigrant, Christian constituency. With only one-fourth of the electorate now professing to be Republicans, it is morphing into a minority party to the disbelief of many.

4 Horses Share the Track

The 1950s were banner years for Elkhorn basketball as teams won several conference titles. Those years witnessed two of the finest players in the school's hardcourt history, three-year starters Toby Clauer from 1949 through the 1951 season, and Gordy Babcock who came along two classes later. Both sharpshooters led the SWANI conference in scoring and garnered all-state mention. Clauer was amply supported by classmate Jerome (Jerry) Hart, and Babcock by a pair of multisport mainstays—Bill Kehoe, and Jerry Welch.

But the sports scene was about to change in 1954 with the addition of track and field. Jon Dahle, science teacher and varsity football coach, hired a year earlier, was encouraged by two of his players, Myron (Mike) Paddock and Richard (Dick) Grimm to start a "thinclad" program. With only baseball and tennis available in the spring, the boys wanted another sport to help them stay in shape for football.

To say that Elkhorn track had an inauspicious beginning in 1954 would be an understatement. Dahle had little knowledge of track and field and no coaching experience. The boys had no running track, no uniforms, and a modicum of equipment, but they were a determined group with a supportive coach.

The Elk thinclads in the 1950s did not have a cinder-based, standard quarter-mile oval track; what they ran on was a 545-yard, irregular, dirt, training road for race horses boarded in the fairground stables. And the county agricultural society that owned the grounds was good enough to allow the track team to use its facilities, when riders were not training pacers and trotters.

Harness racing has a rich history at the fairgrounds where early summer events in July and later during the county fair made up the annual race card. Owners and their horses from Chicago's Maywood, Arlington, and Balmoral Parks made their way to Elkhorn each summer, since 1898, for weekend races that drew thousands of fans in the track's classic grandstand structure.

Paddock secured the family tractor and graded the rough-hewed horse track. Grimm set up shop in the manual arts room and built hurdles. Together they dug high jump, pole vault, and broad jump pits, placed hurdles, and measured the odd-shaped, non-standard running course. Paddock then used the family truck—during the school day—to haul sawdust from Williams Bay for padding in the pits. No inflatable cushions in those days.

The team attracted not only football players, looking for an alternative activity, but boys who had never participated in a varsity sport. Others also apparently derived pleasure from the field event facilities located at the far end of the athletic complex adjacent to a wooded area. Occasionally, the boys would find a condom discarded in the aptly named broad jump pit.

Still, the Elkhorn "track" was more than what most conference schools had, and teams ventured to the county seat for dual and triangular meets. Delavan runners shaped a track of sorts on a barren lot behind a new elementary school. Burlington, who did not field a team in the 1950s, had a quarter-mile oval, albeit in disrepair. Lake Geneva also did not offer the sport until

1959, and Whitewater High, used the college facility at what is now the University of Wisconsin–Whitewater.

The track squads at EHS wore purple gym shorts, white basketball jerseys (with yellow numbers front and back) that had been in storage for several years, gray sweats, and the popular Keds or PF flyers tennis shoes For racing and serious training, Paddock drove the athletic director's car to Madison (again during the school day) and purchased track spikes. While there he also had the coach's stylish auto serviced.

In addition to assisting Coach Dahle, Grimm and Paddock were versatile performers—out of necessity. Dick scaled the high hurdles, high jumped, threw the discus, and tossed the shot, while Mike ran the dashes and low hurdles, broad jumped, and pole vaulted.

A few others were competitive that inaugural year: senior Don Isham, a gutsy miler who went under five minutes (4:53) the same year Roger Bannister broke the 4:00 minute barrier; sprinter and broad jumper Logan Wenger; 880-yard runner, Don Kayser; and Dean Channing, a quarter miler. The team's best athlete was sophomore Bill Ward, a shot-putter, discus thrower, and dash man. Bob Klitzkie and Ralph Morello, also 10th graders, were told by coach Dahle to join the team, if they expected to play football in the fall. During that first 1954 season, the Elk thinclads did not win a single dual meet.

Next year brought the same. As the 1955 spring drew to a close, Jon Dahle convinced the school's athletic director, Lawrence "Bud" Baxter to add a few baseball players to the track roster. Baxter, a fixture at the school during the past two decades and varsity basketball coach, was on the way out. He would be retiring at the end of the school year, prematurely forced out to make room for a younger and more demanding coach. Baxter's slowdown play was giving way to a faster game, and his coaching style was best described as minimalist. Bud Baxter was a gentle man, popular in the community and, with his wife, operated a sporting goods storefront out of their home, but his enthusiasm for coaching seemed to be waning.

Jon Dahle knew that the fastest athletes in school could be found on the baseball field swinging bats, running bases, and chasing down fly balls. The heart of the 1955 baseball team was senior Jim Platts, a hard-throwing pitcher, and four underclassmen: junior shortstop Clarence "Sonny" Colombe and sophomores Bill Riese and Dick Van Scotter along with freshman Roger Van Scotter. Riese and the elder Van Scotter variously roamed the outfield, while the younger Van was the team's second baseman and lead-off hitter.

Platts, perhaps the best athlete in the Southern Lakes Conference, was a standout in both football and basketball as a talented tailback (in Dahle's single-wing offense) and high-scoring guard on the hard court. Riese showed promise that fall as an elusive runner and tenacious defensive back, while the Van brothers held down the backcourt on a prolific, conference champion B team in basketball.

The track season extended beyond baseball play that spring, and Dahle brought the ball players to the track to run in the final dual meet. Earlier the Elks notched two dual meet victories and placed fourth out of six teams in the conference meet. Now, they were hungry for more. With baseball players running various legs, the 880-yard relay team set a school record. In the board jump, sophomore Dick Van would best Paddock's record, and for the only time in his prep career finish ahead of younger brother Roger in the sprints.

This would be a forerunner of future track fortunes at EHS. Dahle had set the stage for athletes to compete in two spring sports, but he would depart Elkhorn at the end of the school year and take a position at Mukwonago High. This was not an upward move for the coach and science teacher, which he was in that order. It was clear to school officials that if the academic program was to improve, the science department needed rejuvenating, just as the athletic department needed a new leader.

5 A New Era Unfolds

The man who doesn't read good books has no
advantage over the man who can't read them.
Mark Twain

Faculty turnover at archetypal small-town schools was commonplace. Young single teachers often would find their first position at a place like Elkhorn then find social life away from the college town in this family-oriented community isolating. Most would move on, but occasionally one would find a marriage partner. In the fall of 1955, Elkhorn High would undergo a faculty overhaul.

Among them were Gordon Hennum, a social studies teacher fresh out of Carroll College in Waukesha; John Lawrence a University of Wisconsin graduate and Dale Lium, from Wisconsin State College—River Falls would head the science department; Arlene Zaffrann, with her B.A from Alverno College in Milwaukee and an English/drama instructor; and Carol Bartingale, English teacher with a newly minted degree also from UW, the state flagship university in Madison. Ward and the Van Scotter brothers, all college material, thrived in the new academic environment. Lium had no ambition to coach, but his no-nonsense instruction was just what the science curriculum needed. In contrast, Hennum's strongest quality was to fill several coaching spots— assistant varsity football, B-team basketball, and head track coach.

Leading the physical education department would be Fred Suchy, who previously had been the varsity football and basketball coaches at Bloomer High School, north of Eau Claire, and Shawano High School, northwest of Green Bay, both in the Northern half of the state. Suchy brought a new t-formation in football and an aggressive yet disciplined brand of basketball to EHS. Players immediately took to the new systems.

In football, it opened quick-hitting pathways for senior Jack Kirkham, Riese, and the Van Scotter brothers, who now were in the varsity backfield. With speed supplied by the underclassmen, Co-captain Ward took over left tackle, fortifying the offensive line, and played middle linebacker on defense. Ralph Morello, the other co-captain that fall, along with Bob Welch, were "bookends" on the frontline, both offense and defense, while senior Bob Klitzkie snapped the ball over center. Sonny Colombe quarterbacked the high-scoring team that tallied a record-setting 199 points over the nine-game schedule.

In basketball, headed by center Klitzkie, players welcomed a fast-break style that heretofore had not been witnessed in Elkhorn. The Van brothers assumed backcourt positions, while seniors Jerry Share and Morello, along with junior Dan Morrow and sophomore, Jon Platts, rounded out the seven players, who consumed most of the playing time that winter of 1955–56. In a couple years, Suchy would produce conference champions and propel Elkhorn to a respected position in the state basketball scene.

That fall, sophomore Roger Van served notice that he would become the premier running back in the conference. Van's speed and quickness, perfect for

Suchy's offense, impressed other players and prompted coaches to design defenses around his threat. Unlike many track sprinters, Van could "cut on a dime" while in full stride with the ball. And his dexterity on the hard court and diamond translated to the gridiron as a lethal pass receiving threat.

As a grade school student, Roger Van displayed extraordinary speed. Even as his brother, older by 11 months and a grade ahead, was outrunning classmates in foot races, Roger could keep up with him. Billy Riese at the time attended Bowers Elementary, a K–8 rural school that fed into Elkhorn for high school, but he likely would have been running stride-for-stride with the Van boys. As for Bill Ward, he was distinguishing himself as a big, strong, fast kid, who was like a man among boys in early adolescence.

Each Halloween, Elkhorn merchants and community organizations sponsored a festival for children at the public school's athletic field. A feature event was a grade-level footrace of 50 or 100–yards with the longer distance reserved for older students. Classmates, citizens, and coaches took notice of the 8th grade race in 1952, when young Roger Van Scotter appeared "shot from a cannon." The race resembled a contest between an Olympic sprinter and a field of chess players. This talent didn't go unnoticed by high school coaches, who would have the kid on their teams the following year.

In the meantime, his brother Richard was recovering from rheumatic fever detected on the final day of the previous school year at the end of 7th grade. Due to the vigilance of his mother and the timely diagnosis by family physician, Dr. Edmund Sorenson, his convalescent period was conveniently just the summer months. Yet, those three months confined to bed were agonizing for the active lad, who, nevertheless, did not miss any school and wasn't set back in his studies. Even then he devised ways to demonstrate to the doctor that his temperature did not creep above normal—98.6 degrees—and that recovery was proceeding smoothly. Such is the indiscretion of a kid, who thinks himself indestructible. Dick Van maintained an upbeat spirit while his athletic activities were put on hold, and his skill development arrested.

A cautious Doc Sorenson kept the lad out of all sports activities in 8th grade, which was understandable but frustrating for the young athlete. During the year, he served as manager and statistician for the junior high school basketball team, "cooling his heels" on the sidelines. As each season approached, Dick Van would convince his parents to pay a visit to the popular doctor hoping to receive a medical release to compete. The football season during his freshman year at the high school came and went with young Van relegated to team manager. This scene was repeated in basketball, as Dr. Sorenson attended every game, where he could insure that coaches did not play the boy.

Edmund Sorenson was a pillar of the community, president of the school board, and respected physician. He had delivered Helen Van Scotter's five boys—not that this in anyway enhanced his medical credentials. He too was the parent of three boys, and the second oldest, Bob, a star player on the conference championship basketball and football teams in 1945 and 1946. The youngest Sorenson boy had been a classmate of Dick Van's during the early elementary grades, but young Joe slipped back to Roger's class.

Joey was learning disabled and today would be given special education treatment. But this was well before the 1975 Education for All Handicapped Children Act (special education), and the boy was merely thought to be amusing but dim. It was observant to a young Dick Van that teachers provided great support for Joey, in part because of the status of his father but also from their inherent compassion for the youngster. Although handled with dignity, Joey's condition likely added to the family stress.

It was known that Mildred Sorenson, Edmund's wife, was a drinker; no doubt, the doctor himself responded to the pressures of life with liquor use, but, if so, it never showed in his professional and civic work. One of Helen Van's abiding personal qualities was to welcome workers to her home for coffee and conversation. Among regular guests in her kitchen was the city sanitation crew who, with other morsels of information, told of intriguing cultural archeology in the village. Based on container content, related the "garbage men," the Sorensons were the largest consumers of "booze" in this town of abundant alcohol drinkers.

Life for a doctor's wife, particularly in a small town, can be difficult, even depressing. Still, it appeared as challenging for the mother of two little girls, who had to manage her inebriated husband, a musician, when he staggered past the Van Scotter dwelling on Washington Street. On more than one occasion, a brother would help the man to his feet and head him in the direction of home. It's possible that today, Joey's condition would be diagnosed "fetal alcohol syndrome." This family history also may have contributed to son Bob's untimely death at age 42.

Like his father, Bob Sorenson was a medical doctor and personal friend of Don Van, second oldest of the brothers. Shortly before his death, Bob attempted to drown himself while scuba diving with Don, who reacted in time to rescue him. This was a classic call for help, and on a subsequent occasion, while alone, Bob Sorenson was successful in his fatal attempt.

At the start of his sophomore season, Dick Van again visited the office of Dr. Sorenson where hopefully he could gain permission to join the football team. His quest once more was rejected, so he contributed to the athletic program by serving as manager for varsity football. In the meantime, younger brother Roger, a freshman, was dazzling opponents, teammates, and fans with his nifty running on the B-team.

In a few months, basketball season approached, and like night follows day, Dick made his trip to see the doctor. This time to his delight, whether for sound medical reasons or just to get the kid out of his office, Doc Sorenson permitted him to join the B-team with one irrevocable condition: that he play four minutes at a stretch then rest for at least another four minutes.

This was a new lease on life for the 15-year-old boy, who also was turning the corner in his academic work and becoming an accomplished student. Heretofore, he was a mediocre, underachieving kid who found most of his studies a distraction from sports and outdoor activities. Yes, there were many rainy fall afternoons and cold winter days, when he would escape to the Matheson Memorial Library near his home and find comfort in books. He particularly enjoyed reading history with its intriguing events, facts, and personalities, but this for the most part took place outside the regular school curriculum. Now, in this sophomore season, he would find his academic stride, so to speak, and welcome challenging assignments, participate in class, and perform at a high scholastic level.

It was a significant transformation for a kid to recognize his innate ability and intellectual curiosity. Some of the change was the natural result of mental and emotional maturity. Still, much of the retardation had to do with the nature of schooling and its effect on an energetic youngster. Social critic, Paul Goodman described this as "Sunday afternoon neurosis." Despite the dedication and patience of elementary teachers, schooling often was a dull sensation for the boy. To paraphrase Goodman, it was a case of "a lively child brought to a pause."

With the realization that someday he must earn a living, which wouldn't be work remotely like his father's trade as a plumber, vocational awareness surfaced. The lad didn't know what career lay ahead, but he did understand that it would require a college education. In the process, he stumbled on to the path to what later he would describe as "scholar, citizen, and artisan."

Young Van responded in the classroom and on the basketball floor. In his 50 percent playing time that translated into 16 minutes per game, he contributed more than many players would over a full game. Not every game was a scoring feast, of course, and he had three teammates who were equally as talented— sophomore Dan Morrow and freshmen Jon Platts along with younger brother Roger. These four would lead the B-team Elks to a conference title that winter and be inseparable teammates for the next three years.

To ensure that Van did not abuse his playing privilege, Dr. Sorenson attended every Elkhorn home game, and many away games, monitoring the boy's playing time. Jon Dahle, this his final season at the school, was the B-team basketball coach. True to his casual style, Dahle permitted Van to self-monitor and voluntarily check in and out of the game every four minutes, thus relieving the coach of this medical imperative. Also true to form, young Van sometimes would stretch four minutes playing time into five, when the thrill of competition was too compelling. And Coach Dahle didn't object.

After every game, Dr. Sorenson would enter the locker room and monitor Dick's heart, comparing his recovery time to Roger's. This worked for player and coach except on the occasion when Dick ignored his playing limits, and the doctor came storming into the locker room chastising player and coach for the potentially health-threatening transgression. This was not the evening that

Van tossed in 23 points going 7 for 9 from the field and 9 for 9 from the charity stripe. Not having developed a jump shot yet, he drove to the basket with abandon. There would be memorable games later on the varsity, but here he scored nearly half of the teams 53 points playing the equivalent of two quarters. Never again would he come so close to perfection on the court.

Two other occasions standout as "nirvana" experiences—one on the football field and the other a 10 kilometer road race. On a picture-perfect autumn afternoon in Cedar Rapids, Iowa, in a 1960 Midwest Conference game against Coe College, Beloit quarterback Jim Kuplic launched a perfect pass that Van caught in full stride for a 90-yard touchdown. No one, not even his brother Roger, would have caught him that afternoon, and certainly not one of the Iowa white boys in Coe's defensive secondary. The other enchanting event took place 20 years later at the Orange Bowl 10 Kilometer race in Coconut Grove, Florida. It was an exquisite December morning, when Van went up against the best master runners (age 40 and over) in the Southeast. For 6.2 miles, he ran a near five-minute per mile pace, appearing stronger with each mile much as a seasoned pitcher would over nine innings of baseball. As he glided the last victorious half mile with the sun rising on the horizon over Biscayne Bay, Van was as close to heaven as he is ever likely to get.

Even at a young age, it occurred to the youngster that physicians were conservative. As Coach Suchy remarked in discouraging a visit to the doctor, "They will tell you to rest, but you are young and will heal fast. Get back on the field." It's in part a liability issue, and doctors protect themselves.

With one semester of biology credit on his transcript, the high school sophomore thought that the doctor was overly cautious. Doc wouldn't let him play football, where frequent rests were the norm, but he did allow basketball a continuous running, stop and start game that seemed more stressful. Also, at the time, medical authorities argued that distance races (with a steady intake and assimilation of oxygen) to be more dangerous than sprints (where powerful bursts of speed place more stress on the cardiovascular system). As medical knowledge on athletic training and competition advanced in coming decades, the intuitive understanding of the youngster proved to be more prophetic than the empirical conclusions of the medical establishment.

Still, for a period of the young man's life, his health rested on a thin thread. This was 1951, and the watchful doctor made house calls every other day to monitor the boy's progress. His fee was based, no doubt, on "ability to pay" and recovered through installments. Compare this with care today, where patients are "fast tracked" through office appointments to aggressively maintain fee-based schedules. Even then, the patient's "opportunity cost" for time spent in the waiting room is considered negligible.

Many youngsters with rheumatic fever had longer recoveries and precarious medical lives. Van was fortunate that he had an alert mother and competent diagnostician in Edmund Sorenson. He also has had the good sense and fortune to lead an active life that both reduced stress and ultimately built a strong cardiovascular system.

6 Scholar Athletes

Education is not filling a pail but lighting a fire.
William Butler Yeats

The term student-athlete is an overused, corrupted term in big-time college sports and increasingly so in high schools. Even as a young student, emphasizing athletics in the absence of classroom excellence seemed fraudulent. Dick Van witnessed this at EHS in the 1950s, as athletes received special attention from staff, faculty, and townspeople. At the end of each year, the high school awarded an American Legion Medal to the top athlete who also was to be an accomplished student. It was Elkhorn's version of recognizing the outstanding student-athlete, but officials "turned a blind eye" when the top athlete in a given year wasn't much of a student.

To Dick Van the intellectual awakening came that sophomore year in the fall of 1954. His class card was filled with demanding courses including algebra, biology, Latin, and English as well as a few rigorous teachers who both stimulated and "held the kid's feet to the academic fire." Science and math brought to life his slumbering analytic aptitude, while Latin, with its ancient stories, gave him an appreciation of language that he had never before experienced. Within the first week of Latin class, Dick Van understood that he did not understand the English language despite having spent the previous 10 years in English-speaking classrooms. Ruth Bushman was an exacting yet compassionate teacher, and the maturing boy's response, fortunately, was to study, participate, recite, and study some more. In time, it was the study of Latin that brought about his appreciation of both the beauty and mechanics of the English language.

With this awakening, he later understood what communications analyst Neil Postman meant when he wrote that "language is the greatest gift we receive from culture." And it is our responsibility, as citizens and human beings, to use it with care and precision. In a few decades, Van would be dismayed how professors, doctors, bankers, financial brokers, and corporate executives—retreat into specialized, impenetrable, verbal enclaves. The British playwright, George Bernard Shaw, described their arcane jargon as a "conspiracy against the public."

One sign of a civilization in trouble, writes essayist John Ralston Saul, is when "its language breaks down into exclusive dialects that prevents communication." The role of responsible, literate elites is to use language "as a daily tool to keep the machinery of society moving" and aid communication. Otherwise, they don't recognize the vital relationship between power and morality and, by standards of Western Civilization, are themselves illiterate.

This foundation acquired in Latin class also would help him navigate the academic contours of Sam Kaplan's challenging sophomore English. Students came to Kaplan's classroom either prepared to participate or prepared to be embarrassed. Embarrassed not because Kaplan was a sadist, but rather learning was the expectation most students brought with them to class.

He was a feared but respected teacher. Every student, every class was called to display their learning, and Kaplan's classroom, pedagogically speaking, was 100 percent "time-on-task."

Dick Van's first encounter with Sam Kaplan was in freshman English. Kaplan led the class to the school library to select a book to read and review. Van located the thinnest available volume and seemingly easiest to read, and took it to the teacher for approval. Mr. Kaplan then gripped his upper arm returning to the stacks, explaining that the boy was ready for something more rigorous. The book Kaplan selected was *Lost Horizon* by James Hilton, the English novelist. The story takes place in the Tibetan borderlands of a southwestern Chinese province in fictitious "Shangri-la." The book initially was beyond the kid's semi-literate comprehension, but he was not about to fall short of Mr. Kaplan's standards. For the next month, many hours were spent trying to understand and write about the novel. This involved Sunday afternoons, secluded upstairs, while Roger and friends played ball outside.

Today, the intellectual process more than the book's content is remembered. Yet, this experience, subliminally, influenced Van's subsequent interest in utopian literature, particularly Edward Bellamy's *Looking Backward.* It also, probably, generated the growth of brain cells that would prove useful in future academic study.

Sam Kaplan arrived daily to school impeccably attired in a stylish suit or sport coat and dress shirt with a classy tie. In his mid-30s, he was physically fit with an olive skin-tone and dark complexion. The man was not classically handsome but fashionable. For him, school was a place of respect and for serious learning. Great teachers are transformative, in that they change a person's life, and Kaplan may have met this criterion for some. For most, however, he offered care and provocation, the mark of a good teacher trying to impart more than just marketable skills and information.

Teachers who matter the most, explains author Mark Edmundson, are not necessarily benevolent. An aspiring thug in high school, Edmundson evolved into a prominent literary critic as a result of a teacher his senior year. "The two greatest teachers we know in the West," he notes, "Socrates and Jesus, were not without kindness ..., but both had a sharp edge." Jesus asked people to give up all their possessions and follow him, to change their lives utterly around, the writer adds. Socrates asked badgering questions to get his contemporaries to live the examined life. In the end, society could not tolerate either man, and did away with them.

It was this grounding during Dick Van's sophomore year and beyond at EHS, that would serve him well throughout the remainder of his formal education and on into life and careers. As Bill Ward remarked shortly before his death, "Some of us had a prep-school education." Those not going to college graduated as literate people with sound vocational skills, assuming they made the effort. All this was a wonderful experience for the young man, opening his eyes to the intellectual and human possibilities of a liberal arts education.

In addition to teaching responsibilities, Kaplan was the baseball coach, and this was to be Dick Van's first season as a starting varsity athlete. He played on the team as a freshman but in a limited apprentice role. Now in the spring of 1955, he was prepared to be the centerfielder, for which he had been rehearsing since grade school. His big-league role model was Philadelphia Phillies' centerfielder Richie Ashburn. Not only did Van often use the playing name "Richie," but the Phillies' speedy contact hitter and base stealer was a model suited for the young ballplayer. The first game in 1955 signaled his potential: Richie Van went three for three with a single, double, and 4ᵗʰ-inning home-run blast over the centerfielder's head. Van was errorless in the field for the season and hit .313, while batting in the fifth position. As a freshman, Roger was the second baseman beginning a varsity career during which he would earn 12 athletic letters.

Sam Kaplan would not remain at EHS. At the request of other coaches, he was relieved of football and basketball duties. He could stay as baseball coach but realized his talents were not appreciated by some staff and resigned. All small school faculties need at least one teacher who is an intellectual force, or face mediocrity.

♪

The 1955-56 year opened with anticipation and promise for the Van brothers. The coaching staff was revamped, and players were greeted that fall by Coach Suchy and assistants Hennum and Lawrence. Dr. Sorenson opened the gates to full athletic participation for Dick Van in his first season of high school football. Bill Ward, a two-year starter at fullback now was moved to the line to make room for the younger and smaller but elusive running backs, particularly Riese and the Van Scotter brothers. And Suchy's new formation fit the Elks to a "T." Roger Van at 135 lbs and quarterback Sonny Colombe at 145 lbs were pound-for-pound the most dangerous and toughest backs, respectively, in the conference. In a first game 46 to 7 romp of Burlington St. Mary's (now Burlington Catholic), Roger Van opened the scoring with a 15-yard dash and Dick Van ended it by returning a punt for a touchdown. The season ended on the same note, as the Elks ran around, through, and over Lake Geneva in a snow storm, 26 to 7.

The homecoming game on a chilled October night was a "mud bath" played in a downpour. The weather "leveled the playing field" and nullified the Elks' speed. After Mukwonago took a 13 to 0 lead, Suchy went to a backup plan and inserted Ward at fullback. The powerful runner hammered at the Indians' line in what would be "four yards and a pile of mud" rather than the proverbial "three yards and a cloud of dust." His pounding distracted linebackers permitting Colombe to hit Welch with a scoring strike and Roger Van to scoot through an opening for a 35-yard sprint to the end zone. With this the Elks were off to the races and a 28 to 13 victory. The "purple and gold" finished third in the conference behind powerhouses Wilmot and Whitewater with a 6-2-1 record. Suchy brought not only a new system to EHS but also new energy.

The Whippets were a nemesis for the Elks on the gridiron during the 1950s, given their "plow horse" backs with "P" names. Harvey Plucinski, Bernie Partol, Daryl Pieper, and especially the Paynters—Bob ('55), Myron ('58), and Arne ('59)—were heavy loads for the lightweight Elks to corral.

Basketball practice started the following Monday, and the players immediately saw that Suchy's practices and style would be much different than in previous years. As with football, sophomores Jon Platts and Roger Van joined the varsity along with juniors Morrow and Dick Van and seniors Klitzkie, Morello, Share, Welch, Colombe, and Fred Stopple. The squad did not challenge for the conference title, but nearly every game was contested. The highlight came in the second half of the season, when the Elks upset highly-ranked Wilmot on its home floor. As the final buzzer sounded, the elder Van triumphantly booted the ball that exploded off his foot and traveled to the gym ceiling like a missile in flight, loosening tiles in the Panthers' new gymnasium and drawing the ire of Wilmot students. The players had to be escorted from the locker room to the team bus that evening. At the season's end, Klitzkie was voted first team all-conference, while Morrow and Dick Van received honorable mention.

Fred Suchy was a facsimile of the basketball coach in the movie *Hoosiers* played by Gene Hackman. Like Norman Dale, Suchy was a talented coach with a checkered past. He had left Shawano High under duress having developed a team that would win the Wisconsin prep basketball tourney—in 1956 and 1957—the first two years after he departed. As a young man, Suchy had a temper that cost him his coaching position. Shawano's loss was Elkhorn's gain. Coach Suchy would find a home in this hub of Walworth County, where his wife Helen and he raised a family of four children and become the most successful basketball coach in the school's history.

Some years later, Dick Van met with Bert Grover, who then was the Wisconsin State Superintendent of Schools in Madison. (That's his real name, and he had pictures of the *Sesame Street* characters—Bert and Grover—on his office door.) Dr. Grover had been a center on the Shawano basketball team during Coach Suchy's last season at the school. Van and the superintendent were meeting for educational purposes, but the first 35 minutes of their conversation focused on the coach and his ill-fated departure from Shawano, which had haunted Grover for years. It was his perceived poor play during a game late in the 1955 season that prompted Suchy to lose his composure, in the locker room, and injure a player. Two decades later, when Elkhorn was making a run at its first state basketball championship, Grover, then superintendent of the Monona Grove schools, opened his high school gymnasium to the coach's hoopsters, where they had a practice session for the tournament. With this, a mantle of guilt was lifted from the superintendent's psyche.

7 Historic Season

We can only be said to be alive in those moments
when our hearts are conscious of our treasurers.
Thornton Wilder

The spring of 1956 would be an historic season for the Elkhorn thinclads. Football and basketball teams typically dressed out in stylish "purple and gold" with white uniforms reserved for home contests. In 1956, and for the next few seasons, the same could not be said for the track team. The most generous description of the track outfits is to say that they were "vintage" gear. There was nothing subtle or veiled about those uniforms and certainly nothing "thin" about them; they looked exactly like what they were—gym shorts and old basketball singlet. And the boys sported old-fashioned spiked running shoes. But none of this bothered the more than 20 runners who reported for practice.

Every spring weekend was fair and sun-filled. The track season opened in grand fashion as the Elks triumphed over Delavan and East Troy with both Van Scotter brothers leaping over 20 feet and exceeding the broad jump record—later renamed long jump to avoid a tacit sexual reference. A few weeks later when the state track and field rankings were published, Roger Van had the Class B top performances in both the broad jump (21'3") and 220-yard dash (22.0). Distances then were measured in yards not meters, and the size of the fairgrounds' track permitted the 220 to be run on the straightaway. Track and field aficionados took notice of the swift sophomore.

Big invitational meets were a new experience for Elkhorn track, so the boys participated with a sense of awe and anticipation. Rules governing Wisconsin interscholastic track and field in the 1950s contained limitations and restrictions: the longest running distance was 1-mile, the 300-meter hurdles had not yet replaced 180-yard low hurdles, and the culminating relay race was the 4 x 220-yard (or 880-yard) relay. Until 1956, this was the only relay event on the race ticket, outside of designated relay meets. For dual and triangular meets, individuals were limited to competing in four events, including a relay leg, and no more than two running or two field events. For conference meets, sectional qualifying, and the State Track and Field Championship, the restriction was one less event.

In 1956, the Elks "thinclads" included runners, jumpers, and throwers that for the first time could win meets and score points in larger relay and invitational events. The squad was runner-up to Wilmot at the conference finals (though the relay team did beat the Panther's in a thrilling duel) but didn't enter a big-time meet until the sectional competition in late spring.

The Elks approached the sectional meet in Fort Atkinson with great anticipation but modest expectations. Riese, Ward, the Van Scotter brothers, and quarter-miler Dean Channing would receive their severest tests. Roger had set a conference record, winning the 220-yard dash a week earlier and anchored the relay team, so he was not permitted to compete in the 100-yard dash, in which his brother finished second to Wilmot's Don Timmer, one of the state's premier Class C dash men.

Elkhorn, with a slightly larger enrollment was classified in the B division, as were Whitewater, Delavan, and Mukwonago. East Troy joined Timmer and teammates in the lower division.

When the results were tallied, Roger Van had qualified in the 220-yard dash, setting a sectional record on the turn with a time of 22.6. Dick Van and Channing just missed qualifying with third place finishes in their events, but the 800-yard relay team of Riese, Dick Van, Ward, and Roger Van raced to victory over host Fort Atkinson. Ed Sandvold, Fort's anchor runner and defending state 440-yard champion, could offer only amazement after Van opened the lead over him even though running the turn in an outside lane.

This would be the first time in school history that Elkhorn would qualify athletes for state competition in any sport. It was a formidable showing for the track novices with the "uncharted waters" of 1956 State Track and Field Championships in Madison ahead the following week. Roger Van had posted the state's fastest Class B 220 time, while ranked high in both the 100-yard dash and broad jump, and the relay team recorded one of the state's fastest qualifying times. But "all bets were off" at the finals in Madison the following week.

Saturday, May 25, 1956 was a beautiful day at Camp Randall Stadium. As the Elkhorn boys walked out of the UW basketball field house on to the cinder track, shot put and discus action was underway in the infield. The Class A throwers looked huge to kids from Elkhorn unaware that several of these athletes would be Big Ten lineman the following fall. Then the races began with the sound of the starter's gun echoing around the massive football stadium. In 1956, the cinder track still ringed the gridiron at Camp Randall and wouldn't be dug up to increase stadium seating capacity until after the 1957 track season.

In the 1950s, there were no qualifying rounds for relay events. Apparently, high school athletes were thought to need protecting from perceived dangers of excessive competition and zealous coaches. One final event with three heats would determine the results of the 880-yard relay with a team's place based on time. This didn't faze the Elkhorn runners who sat in the vast stadium taking in the competition and enjoying the sight of Alan Ameche, Wisconsin's 1954 Heisman Trophy recipient, then fullback with the Baltimore Colts. Ameche, who had been a football star and trackman at Kenosha High School in the early 1950s, was viewing the events from on high with his entourage of friends.

None of this appeared to unnerve or impress unflappable Roger Van as he set sail in his qualifying round of the 220-yard dash. With the sound of the gun resonating, Van took charge of the race in the first 100 yards, came out of the turn with a sizable lead cruising to victory with a new Class B record of 22.6. With the 880-yard relay the last event of the day, Elk runners went to lunch at a nearby diner where Roger Van consumed wheat germ while Ward, Riese, and Dick Van enjoyed a light meal monitored by Coach Hennum.

Shortly, after returning to the stadium, the finals of the 220-yard dash would be held with Roger going against defending champion Alan Schoonover from Boscobel, a town of about 2,500 residents resting in the southwestern corner of the state. Schoonover was a 6'3" senior and football star headed for the Badgers' gridiron the following fall. Ameche and friends, focused on the big running back, were "blown away" when the 5'8" Elk speedster left the Boscobel flash, peering through flying cinders at his purple shorts and fading basketball numerals. Roger Van had lowered his time to 22.5 and recorded the first of several state track "golds" to be won over the next three seasons.

Coaches from across the state had read about the Elkhorn youngster that spring, but few had seen him compete. The lone sophomore champion among competitors on a balmy afternoon in Madison left observers buzzing about young Van's potential over the next two years. Less than an hour later, the Elk foursome made their way down the stadium steps to the infield, where they would lace-up the well-worn spikes and prepare for the relay event. A critical part of this warm-up routine was to practice a few baton exchanges at full speed. This preparation had been learned well and executed to perfection by the team. It is a critical aspect of the race that seemed instinctual, as if they were born to run relay races and had been doing so over the years on Elkhorn's playgrounds.

Running the opening leg, Riese got a strong start from the third lane position and was holding his own coming out of the turn. The sight of his teammate approaching in a pack of runners was unusual for Dick Van awaiting the hand off of the baton for the second leg of the relay. He was used to Riese having a lead and taking the baton on a clear track. But not today as the Elks faced their stiffest competition of the season. Yet, concentration was one skill that Van learned well from his coaches. In basketball, Fred Suchy emphasized focusing on the front of the rim for free throws, tuning out spectators and players alike and repeating the mantra "over the rim and in." It worked on the court as Van made 80 percent of his "charity" tosses. And it also would be successful on the track. Coach Hennum emphasized ignoring the rest of the field and spotting one's teammate steaming down the track.

At just the right moment, Van took off, dropped back his hand, and snagged the baton at full speed. At sectional and state competition, runners were required to stay in their lanes, so there was no jostling for position as the boys raced for the far turn of the track within the impressive stadium with its scoreboard looming overhead. One of teams in their heat was Menasha, a working class community located at the upper end of Lake Winnebago, in the midst of Wisconsin's paper manufacturing industry. The town Menasha is inevitably mentioned in concert with its neighbor Neenah, as in "Neenah-Menasha," but the socio-economics of the two communities are worlds apart. Paper company executives and management reside in upper-middle-class Neenah, while blue-collar workers make their homes in Menasha. Over the years, Neenah high school excelled in basketball and tennis, while Menasha fielded strong football and track teams. And 1956 was no exception; Menasha High was one of the top football teams in the state that fall, and three members of its backfield were relay runners, who also participated in individual sprint events at the state meet this day.

Two runners were senior Dick Celichowski and junior Jerry Sobiesczyk, classic family names in central Wisconsin's industrial towns. In a couple years, Dick Van would meet up with Celichowski, as a shifty running back and sprinter for Ripon College. The anchor leg runner for Menasha was junior Tom Hyde, who had captured the 100-yard dash earlier in the meet. In a couple years, Hyde would go on to the University of Iowa where he played football and ran track. The Menasha foursome went into the finals with the fastest Class B relay time that spring. Over the next two years, Elkhorn High would pride itself in having the fastest football backfield in the state made up of the track relay team. But in 1956, this honor went to Menasha.

As Dick Van came out of the turn two-thirds of the way through his leg of the relay, he was stride-for-stride with several other runners. At the exchange, he held his own with the fast field, but the Menasha high flyers had opened up a lead, which they lengthened during the third leg. Nevertheless, the pass between Dick Van and Ward was flawless, and the 195 lb. senior, churned cinders as he made his way around the third turn of the race. Ward, a tackle and linebacker on the football team, may have been the fastest shot putter in the state, but on this day he would lose a couple precious yards to the leaner Menasha runner.

Again, Ward executed a crisp exchange with Roger Van, who was in the middle of the field. This was a new and wonderful experience for the nascent Elkhorn foursome, who was hoping to grab a place in the event and add at least two points to their team total. In short order, Roger Van sprinted from the field, but Menasha had created an insurmountable gap for Hyde that Van could not entirely close. Menasha's time was 1:34.1 with Elkhorn in their wake at 1:34.4. But this was only one of three heats, and the inexperienced Elks had little idea what fate the other two heats would bring. They only knew they could place no higher than second.

Soon the event drew to a close, and the results announced: Sturgeon Bay, a school located in the state's beautiful Door County just north of Green Bay, would equal Elkhorn's time, but no other team could. On this magnificent spring afternoon in Madison, the EHS "purple and gold" thinclads were awarded seven points (splitting the difference with Sturgeon Bay between second and third place) to add to the five points earned by Roger Van in winning the 220-yard event.

Wisconsin track and field then awarded double points in relay events, so first-place finishers, for example, received 10 points as opposed to five for individual events. In the 1950s, only five places scored points in both individual events and relays. Today, as many as eight individuals and teams are awarded points in major meets with winners earning ten. Because of this and the larger number of events, e.g., four relays as opposed to two, point totals tend to be substantially higher.

This wasn't a state championship for Elkhorn yet; the 12-point total gave them seventh-place in the overall standings in 1956. Greendale, a Milwaukee suburb, claimed the Class B title with 19 points, while Menasha and Platteville were next with 17 points. But it was a defining moment in Elkhorn sports history and turning point in its embryonic track program. As the coach and five teammates made their way back to town late that afternoon, they pondered what was ahead for Elkhorn track fortunes. Ward, who would be graduating in a few days, exclaimed that this was the highlight of his scholastic sports and proudest moment in his athletic life.

During Bill's boyhood, his father passed away, and his older sister, younger brother, and he would be raised by his mother. Yet, as he related prior to death from stomach cancer 50 years later, it was the community of Elkhorn that raised him. Before his sophomore year, Bill's mother, who had failing health, moved to Milwaukee with younger brother Jim to be near her family. Bill and his sister, Mary Ann, remained behind to finish high school in Elkhorn, where he lived with the Klitzkie family and teammate Bob, whose father also had died a few years earlier.

At the high school graduation ceremony that spring, Bill Ward earned academic honors and the American Legion Medal as top student-athlete. Elkhorn sports never realized how it might have benefited had younger brother Jim, a classmate of Roger Van, remained in town. He would become a star athlete at Milwaukee Washington High, qualifying for the State Class A meet in the hurdles. Jim was as fast as his older brother, and, at 6'4", several inches taller. Bill went on to Whitewater for college studies, and Jim matriculated to the University of Wisconsin where he was a varsity heavyweight wrestler. After college, Bill joined the Navy and entered Officer Candidate School, there upon spending several years on the high seas, another venture that Dick Van and he held in common. In time, Bill Ward married and came to live in central Pennsylvania, where he taught college and raised a family.

In 2001, 45 years later, Dick Van and daughter Shannon travelled to The Netherlands and toured the countryside by bicycle. One stop, about 60 miles out of Amsterdam, was the town of Bunschoten, where their ancestors once lived. The family name "van Bunschoten" was changed over generations to "Van Scotter." About a three-day trip on two wheels southwest from Bunschoten is the town of Schoonhoven, where the Boscobel sprinter's forebears likely had lived. The "flying Dutch" progeny made their mark on the track that memorable May afternoon in 1956.

2. Elkhorn Cornet Band 1910 – Fred MaGill (row 2, second from right, holding trombone, and Will MaGill (bottom row, seated far right)

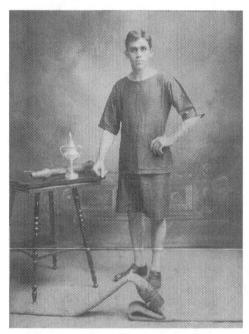

3. Fred MaGill fire hose race champion (1902) with running shorts in style a century later.

4. 1906 High School, foreground, and 1887 School, background

5. Early Players—Richie age 4, Roger age 3

6. Band Shell in the Courthouse Square Park

7. County Fair Grandstands and Sulky Races, circa
    1910

8. Downtown Walworth Street and Sprague Theater, 1965

9. Dr. Edmund Sorenson

10. Elkhorn School Board 1956 left to right – Robert Reid, Perry Spenser, Clarence Schacht (Superintendent), Edmund Sorenson (President), Curtis Weaver, Gilbert Church, and Robert MaGill

11. Inaugural Track Team 1954, Bottom row: Dave Fink, Roger Bothe, Larry Hutton, Larry Yanke, Lee Zanin, Gene Anderson, Paul Paddock, and Don Kayser; Middle row: Don Isham, Logan Wenger, Bill Ward, Don Henderson, Dean Channing, Bob Gregerson, Mike Paddock, Coach Jon Dahle; Top row: Dick Grimm, Tom Baker, Tom Reedy, Bob Klitzkie, Ralph Morello, Carl Nelson, Dave Anderson, and Dave Bartleson

12. Football co-captains 1955—Ralph Morello (46) and
    Bill Ward (52) with head coach Fred Suchy and
    assistant coach Gordon Hennum, standing

Jim Platts

Bob Van Scotter

Alan Van Scotter

13. Platts and Van Scotter often were uttered in the same sentence. Jon Platts and Roger Van (class of '58) were the only twosome to be awarded the American Legion Medal. Here Jim Platts ('55), Bob Van ('46), and Alan Van ('62) wear #35 at the time popular numerals for star running backs emulating Army's Felix "Doc" Blanchard and Wisconsin's Alan "the Horse" Ameche.

14. Don "Tiny" Millard, 6'7" center on 1945-46 championship team.

15. 1947 basketball—top to bottom, Bob Sorenson, Frank Eames, and Bob Hanny

16. Halfbacks 1955, sophomore Roger Van (21) and
junior Dick Van (20)

17. 1955-56 Basketball Starters (photographed from balcony of the 1906 gym): left to right, Jerry Share, Dan Morrow, Bob Klitzkie, Ralph Morello, Dick Van Scotter, and Roger Van Scotter

18. 220-yard finals, State Meet in Madison, 1956: Roger Van Scotter (21) with Allen Schoonover (Boscobel) far left.

19. Sophomore sprinter, Roger Van Scotter

20. Baseball 1956, Dick Van Scotter

21. 1956 Relay team in 1940s basketball tops: Bill Riese (56), Dick Van (22), Bill Ward (58), and Roger Van (21)

22. E Club 1956 – Row 1: Dick Van Scotter, Clarence Colombe, Bob Welch, Coach Fred Suchy, Ralph Morello, Bill Ward. Row 2: Leon Lauderdale, Louis Vogt, Dave Fink, Lyle Kyle, Roger Van Scotter, John Martin, Don Walter. Row 3: Ken Brockman, Lee Zanin, Jack Kirkham, Jerry Share, Dick Mann, Bill Riese, Bruce Mitchell. Row 4: Mike Kelley, Jon Platts, Bob Klitzkie, Carl Nelson, Dan Morrow, Don Kayser

23. Underclassmen 1956: left to right, Jon Platts, Roger Van, Dick Van, and Dan Morrow

Southern Lakes

8 Southern Lakes

There is no cure for birth and death except to enjoy the interval.
George Santayana

1 956 was historic for the Southern Lakes Conference in state track: it was the first time a conference athlete had participated in the meet, and rival Wilmot too would shine in the Class C division. Sprinter Don Timmer was nipped at the tape in the 100-yard dash by New Holstein's Bob Dosch, then later anchored the Panthers' 4 x 220-yard relay team to a second place finish in that division. The Wilmot standout that day was senior Ray Arndt, a multi-talented athlete, who won the Class C high hurdles.

The Panthers finished second overall to New Holstein, an east central pastoral community, who ran up 29 points to Wilmot's 20. Timmer, a strapping halfback, would enter Marquette University the following fall and join the football team. Other members of Wilmot's relay team were footballers Ron Faber, Don Schwartz, and junior Dick Timmer, a four-sport star who would follow his older brother to Marquette.

Delavan's half-miler, Phil Reader enhanced the Southern Lakes' reputation with a second place finish in the Class B 880-yard run. In Class C, quarter miler

Lee Ketterhagan, East Troy, and miler Jim Bauman, Wilmot, took fourth place in their respective events. The Southern Lakes had served notice that it would be making a splash in state track in future years.

The Southern Lakes Conference is one of longest running in the state, formed in 1953, and aptly named. During the fifties, it included eight schools: Burlington Demons, Delavan Comets, East Troy Trojans, Elkhorn Elks, Lake Geneva Resorters, Mukwonago Indians, Whitewater Whippets, and Wilmot Panthers.

This is a land of many lakes. When the Wisconsin glacier, the last of four glacier movements on the North American continent, receded about 12,000 years ago northward toward the Arctic Circle, it left a landscape laced with lakes and rolling hills. This fertile land and Nordic beauty attracted industrious northern Europeans and those of Scandinavian descent as a wave of immigration swept across America's Northwest Territory during the 1800s.

Whitewater Lake lies near the town that took its name, as does Delavan Lake, in their respective townships by the same names. These two original SL cities also contained lakes within or near their boundaries: Whitewater claimed Tripp, Cravath, Rice, and Turtle Lakes, along with Lake Lorraine, while Delevan encompassed Comus Lake.

The P.T. Barnum Circus ("Greatest Show on Earth") was founded in Delavan in 1871. The Ringling Brothers, who raised their first tents about 100 miles away in Baraboo, Wisconsin, also found winter quarters in Delavan for its performers and clowns. The surrounding pastures made suitable homes for the circus' valuable horses, elephants, and other animals. During the circus "hayday" from 1847 to 1891, Delavan was home to 26 companies.

The "grand lady" of lakes in the county is Geneva Lake that measures 7.6 miles in length and 2.1 miles at its widest point with a circumference of 21 miles. In summer months, the city of Lake Geneva is a playground for swimmers, water skiers, and boaters prompting the label "Newport of the West." This community of about four thousand residents in 1950, and nearly ten thousand today, swells to triple that number in the summertime, as tourists arrive from metropolitan Chicago, Milwaukee, and elsewhere.

Railroad travel between Chicago and Lake Geneva dates to 1871 bringing a stream of people from the Windy City. Al Capone and other mobsters found the town a convenient retreat, while Hugh Hefner made a statement in establishing a Playboy Club there. For many years, P.K Wrigley, the chewing gum magnate, also made his home along the road that circumnavigates Geneva's lakefront. Guns N' Roses lead singer Axl Rose was among other "high rollers" to find solace here.

Just north of Lake Geneva is Lake Como, a fisherman's paradise and small community, whose youngsters have been bused both to Elkhorn and Lake Geneva Badger High.

East Troy, with Mukwonago, Burlington, Wilmot, also are surrounded by lakes that grace their communities and provide "built-in" recreation. Lake Beulah rests on the edge of East Troy, the only other of these four schools wholly in Walworth County. Nearby are small lakes: Booth, Swan, Army, Lulu, and Potter. Nestled south of East Troy en route to Elkhorn and Lake Geneva are the rolling hills of Alpine Valley, a popular outdoor venue for winter skiers and summer music lovers.

Mukwonago, a few miles to the northwest on the border in Waukesha County, includes among its natural assets, the scenery and recreation of Phantom Lake with its intriguing name. Youngsters from across the area attend the summer YMCA camp on this lake.

Burlington, to the south just in Racine County, with Browns Lake near its city limits, is traversed by the Fox River that drifts farther south through Wilmot. In 1835, Burlington was co-founded by Moses Smith, a member of the Latter Day Saints (Mormons). Nearby, in the community of Voree on the White River, James Strang started his Mormon denomination in 1844.

Down the dusty road in Elkhorn, Oliver Cowdery, second to LDS leader Joseph Smith, served as a lawyer and co-editor of the *Walworth County Democrat*. The Belfry theater, originally a Mormon meeting house built in 1888, became a popular summer stock playhouse on route 67 near Williams Bay. Here Paul Newman got his start on stage. In exchange for a room at the Lazy Cloud Lodge, he mowed the lawn.

Although Wilmot High has grown substantially over the past half century, to over 1000 students, the town itself is unincorporated. Most of its students reside in surrounding lake communities that have grown significantly: Silver Lake with its satellite "ponds"—Peat and Rock; Camp, Center, and Lillie Lake; Powers Lake and Benedict Lake, as well as the Twin Lakes—Elizabeth and Mary. Nearby are Paddock, Tombeau, and Cross lakes. Settled near the Illinois border, Wilmot boasts a ski resort, the Kenosha County Fair, and Wilmot Speedway, but most famously it is the home of Wisconsin's oldest restaurant and pub, Wilmot Stage Stop, founded in 1848, the year of statehood.

The city acquired its name from the Wilmot Proviso, a rider to an appropriations bill in 1846, as part of negotiations to resolve the Mexican-American War. Named after Democratic Congressman David Wilmot, the bill, had it passed, would have prohibited slavery in any territory acquired from Mexico. Nevertheless, it is considered one the first events on the slide to secession and the Civil War that intensified during the 1850s. In honor of this legacy, the school, which dates to 1870, took the name Wilmot Free Union.

Elkhorn is the only town in the original Southern Lakes Conference that does not count at least one natural lake among its attractions and resources. Yet, the city is surrounded by about 15 lakes within a 15-mile radius, so citizens of this landlocked town have ample recreation related to water. North of town lay three relatively small lakes – Pleasant, Silver, and one with the whimsical label Wandawega. Given all the wonderful Indian names that grace the region, this should not seem so fanciful. North Lake also is not far away in the northwest quadrant of Sugar Creek Township. The most prominent lakes near Elkhorn are a chain with names Green, Middle, and Mill—collectively called Lauderdale Lakes. In the 1950s, over half of the Elkhorn High students lived in the vicinity of these lakes and within the rural townships of the district's attendance area.

9 To the Baseball Diamond

America will be remembered for three things:
The Constitution, Jazz, and Baseball
Historian, Ken Burns

By the time the state track meet rolled around, the baseball season had drawn to a close. The sport had a modest tournament in the 1950s; nothing like the intensity of Badger basketball, with just eight teams making the trip to Madison each March, nor the individual meritocracy of track and field, where only the swift and strong survive until late May. And the baseball gray uniforms with red trim, though not the school's purple and gold colors and likely acquired at a fire sale, were an upgrade from track threads.

While EHS track records in 1956 were being tossed aside like so many ten pins at the Elk bowling alley on the corner of Geneva and Wisconsin, Riese and the Van Scotter brothers were displaying skills on the baseball diamond. It was an unremarkable season for EHS-nine who had a .500 record over the 10-games, yet the track speedsters displayed their wares on the diamond as well. While the team as a whole batted a tepid .228, Bill Riese and Roger Van were among the top hitters in the conference with .300 plus batting averages. The

Elk's offense too often consisted of Roger Van and Riese getting on base while Dick Van drove them home. The elder Van had a league leading 12 RBIs that spring while batting .476, also the Southern Lakes' best. Extrapolate this RBI-to-games ratio over a 154-game major league season, and the numbers become impressive.

A typical outing was the Wilmot game late in the season, when the Panthers' Dick Timmer, took a no-hitter into the seventh and final inning. With one out on the home team, this had the making of a disaster for Coach John Lawrence's squad. But Roger Van and Bill Riese had managed to get on base through a walk and infield error, and then pulled off a double steal. Dick Van followed to the plate and extended the count on Timmer, who was eager to chalk up a no-hitter and finish off a notable sports year for the Panthers. The hard-throwing right-hander attempted to fire a fastball by Van, which was like the rising morning sun trying to sneak past a rooster. Van kept his hitting streak alive with a shot to the gap in left-center field, scoring two runs.

This was hardly a "walk off" hit as the talented Panthers pounded a couple Elk hurlers. Wilmot was the class of Southern Lakes in 1955-56 whose multi-sport athletes had such surnames as Arndt, Benedict, Bruenning, Faber, Faeber, Haase, Partenheimer, Schilz, Schwartz, Skora, and Timmer. Needless to say, Wilmot was an area settled by hearty German farmers. As Van departed the playing field, Coach Lawrence quietly thanked him for saving his team from an embarrassing no-hitter that gloomy afternoon.

It was a good year for pitchers in the Southern Lakes with only Wilmot having a respectable .290 team batting average. Often those pitchers were three-sport stars and the dominant athlete in their respective schools, as Jim Platts had been the prior three years at Elkhorn High. Besides Dick Timmer, Wilmot also could throw at opponents Ed Skora a tackle in football and center on the hard court, who tossed the shot put and discus. Making Skora and Timmer more menacing on the mound was catcher Don Timmer, all-conference halfback and sprint star. Whitewater mound duties were led by 6'3" junior Charlie Regez, end on the football team and the Southern Lakes leading scorer in basketball that winter. Likewise, East Troy's John and Ted Menne and Delavan's Mike Skopec were the aces of their pitching staffs along with being standouts in football and basketball. As for the Elks, Jim's brother Jon served that role from 1956 to 1958.

Missing in the public works "stimulus package" during the Great Depression was a baseball park to accompany the new high school erected in 1938. The EHS baseball field consisted of make-shift bleachers, dirt infield, and a "do-it-yourself" scoreboard. When a batter connected on the "sweet spot" of the bat, there was no home-run trot to enjoy, because there was no outfield fence for the blast to clear. Instead, the batter had to "high-tail it" on a 120-yard dash (360 feet) around the bases.

The two Van brothers did this with speed and quickness that seemed to have genealogical roots. Fred MaGill, the plumber who played the trombone in the original Holton Band, also was a city fireman and the boys' maternal grandfather. Grandpa had been an accomplished runner himself in a distinctive way. Born in 1875, MaGill became fire chief in 1902, during which time he competed in various fireman contests. One such event, during the days of horse-drawn fire wagons, involved coupling hoses and running a specified distance. He won the Wisconsin Fireman's Tournament in Portage that year and then represented the state in the national contest at the 1903 Louisiana World Exposition in St. Louis, where he finished third.

During a summer season in the early 1950s, city maintenance crew circled the outfield with a burnt-orange wooden snow fence to accommodate fly balls off the bat of Don Breidenbach ('45) and turn them into home runs. Breidenbach was one of two EHS athletes to play minor league baseball; the other being Bob Hanny ('48). Both players were in the Chicago Cubs farm system, but neither made it to Wrigley Field, except when Breidenbach died. After slogging around the minor-leagues for three seasons and reaching Class A Wichita, he joined the city merchants' team. And he could hit a baseball, so up went the fence, which at least on one occasion came down when a jumbo outfielder from Milton crashed through it trying to bring in one of the smooth-swinging slugger's fly balls.

Unfortunately, for the young boys, the shortstop went to college after that summer, and took with him his saucy, pin-up girl friend, Jean, who would sunbath down the right-field foul line during games. Normally, those too young to play on the city team found a seat along the home-team third-base line, but not this summer. The fervent pubescent boys manned the first-base sidelines and could barely attend to the game with the sun-tanned, curvaceous beauty sprawled on her recliner. She looked like a model out of the 1940s with a sassy attitude to match.

Fast forward a few decades when the marriage between the dazzling couple ended with her reportedly leaving for a woman. Don Breidenbach was a proud man who died in his early sixties. His daughters Toni and Tami traveled to Chicago, arrived at the "friendly confines" on the corner of Clark and Addison, and convinced groundskeepers to spread the slick fielder's ashes on the infield at Wrigley Field.

Don Breidenbach and Roger Van shared a fascination of roaming the shortstop position in a Cub's uniform at Wrigley Field. In the recreation room of his home in Laguna Beach, California, the dexterous dentist constructed a replica of Wrigley Field, complete with ivy-vines on the outfield wall and towering scoreboard, with team pennants unfurled, in centerfield. One obstacle to this dream for both EHS ballplayers was a guy named Ernie Banks, aka "Mr. Cub," who broke into the major leagues in 1953 and held down the position for more than a decade.

A little-known fact in the city's history is John Raleigh, its only major league ballplayer. Raleigh, born in 1887 in Elkhorn, was a left-handed pitcher for the St. Louis Cardinals in 1909. Although he had a respectable 3.79 earned run average (ERA), his one win and 10 losses didn't help the then lowly Redbirds who recorded only 54 victories that season. He played a few games in 1910, after which his major league career ended.

Nineteen fifty-six was a wonderful sports year for Elkhorn High: Sonny Colombe, Bill Ward, and Bob Welch were all-conference in football; in basketball Bob Klitzkie was runner up for the league scoring title, while Dick Van won the Southern Lakes batting crown; and Roger Van began his three-year assault on school, conference, and state track records.

10 No Ordinary Town

The free thinking of one age is the common sense of the next.
Matthew Arnold, English Poet

Elkhorn has made the national news in intriguing ways. Roger Touhy, a Chicago racketeer, was captured in July 1933 after he and his men hit a pole on private property outside of town. The owner called the county sheriff's department in Elkhorn, and the car was stopped as it entered town by rookie Harry Ward, a traffic policeman and Bill's distant uncle. The men, who had been on a fishing excursion in upstate Wisconsin, were headed toward the Elkhorn area where "Terrible Tommy" O'Connor, an escaped convict and cop killer, had fled and probably ran Touhy's Wisconsin operation. The men were taken in to pay $22 for damages, where Touhy, worth millions, made the mistake of arguing for half the amount. While he and his men Guy Schaeffer, William Sharkey, and Tom (the Father) McFadden were detained, Ward conducted an illegal search. Digging deep under the front seat cushions of the upscale, high-powered car, the rookie cop found four .38 Colt revolvers, a .45 Colt, a .38 Colt automatic rigged to fire as a machine gun, and a .38 Smith and Wesson rifle.

A phone call was made to the FBI in Chicago who identified the men as the notorious Touhy gang. FBI special agent Melvin Purvis told Elkhorn police to find an excuse to hold the men longer, while he and an army of FBI agents, Chicago detectives, reporters, and news photographers made the two-hour drive to Elkhorn. Touhy later was convicted, spent time in a penitentiary, and, in 1959, was gunned down in a gangland killing reportedly by Al Capone's men.

On a less dangerous yet dramatic note, the Sprague Theater in downtown Elkhorn hosted the movie premier of *Tillie the Toiler* in August 1941, based on a popular comic strip and remake of a 1927 movie. The film's star was a young actress and local girl, Kay Harris, whose movie career was short-lived, but not before she performed in several more films between 1941 and 1943, including *Lucky Legs* (1942) and *The Fighting Buckaroo* (1943). Ms. Harris and her family made their theater entrance to the glow of spotlights and exploding flash bulbs. Earlier, it was the Princess Theater, renamed by owner Dan Kelliher after the Sprague Opera House that had once stood on a nearby corner. The 1940s was an era defined in part by the gracious beauty of young women and film stars. Had Ms. Harris' film career not been so short, and her health fragile (she died in 1971 at age 53), she might be remembered today along with Lana Turner, Rita Hayworth, or at least Jean Arthur, and other striking actresses of the era.

In 1952, the town was the focus of a half hour March of Time TV series entitled "Christmas Time in Elkhorn." The crew spent a month filming aspects of life in a picturesque small town. When artist Cecile Johnson visited the city in the 1950s, she was so charmed by holiday scenes from the court house square that she painted several water colors. The paintings were featured in *Ford Times* magazine and later became the cover for a popular Christmas card series. With this, Elkhorn became known as *The Christmas Card Town.*

In keeping with its conservative tradition, resident Harry H. Tubbs ran unsuccessfully for governor of Wisconsin during the early 1900s on the Prohibition ticket.

Growing up for a small-town kid in the 1950s heartland came with its share of boredom and dull moments. Even today "Sunday afternoon neurosis" is an accurate portrayal of life in most towns. In response, many men numb themselves with football, golf, and other TV sports programming. As Erma Bombeck observed, "If a man watches three football games in a row, he should be declared legally dead." It wasn't until Dick Van's San Francisco experience that he appreciated the vitality of urban Sunday afternoons.

Nevertheless, the fifties were "Happy Days" as depicted in the popular 1970s TV series. The cast in the fictitious comedy show, set in Milwaukee, had its real life counterpart characters in cities and towns around Wisconsin and many other places. Every community could identify its Arthur (Fonzie) Fonzarelli, Richie Cunningham, and feisty little sister Joanie. Cities, small and large, also had their "Arnold's Drive-in" where kids in leather and letter jackets gathered after the Friday Night football and basketball games. In Elkhorn, this popular spot was the aptly named "Slide Inn" located in the bend on Highway 12 near the city limits north of town. Black leather jackets, blue jeans, and swept-back ducktail hair styles were popular among young men, just as flowing skirts, cashmere sweaters, and pony tails were among young women. And a number of EHS coeds were facsimiles of the principle characters in "Laverne and Shirley," the "Happy Days" spin-off sitcom.

In the summertime, merchants kept downtown retail stores open Friday evenings, and folks gathered for "concerts in the park." During the fall season, Harris Memorial Field behind the high school overflowed with spectators for "football under the lights," while in the winter months, they packed the Kinne Gymnasium for basketball. These games were community events, and nearly everybody in town followed the fortunes of the Elks.

Full stands at the football park didn't bother young kids and many men who followed play up and down field, crowding end lines when their team was in the "red zone." On basketball nights near courtside and down a flight of stairs was the home team's locker room. At its entrance and adjacent to the manual arts shop, men gathered during the halftime for a "smoke" and analysis of first-half play. When players departed their quarters heading back to the game floor, they waded through a haze left by the exhaust of burning Camels, Chesterfields, and Lucky Strikes.

Elkhorn's downtown movie house, the Sprague Theater, also had its evening routines. Saturdays and Sundays were reserved for blockbuster films, particularly musicals, of the period that appealed to a traditional adult audience. What today we might refer to as independent or non-mainstream films were reserved for midweek. But Fridays were "kids night" when Roy Rogers, Gene Autry, The Lone Ranger, or other Westerns with celluloid "good guys" and "bad guys" beckoned the town's children. The Friday night ticket price for kids Mr. Kelliher charged was nine cents with his profit coming largely from sales of pop corn, sodas, and candy. The nine-cent ticket price remains a mystery, but surely tellers at the town's two banks were busy counting pennies, nickels, and dimes the following Monday.

♪

That theater is gone, at least for movies, and like many other neighborhood film houses, it was chased away by high costs and multiplexes that dot the national landscape. Today the county has a couple mid-size theaters that appeal mostly to a youth population. Viewers who want a film experience outside mainstream fare are required to travel to Milwaukee or Madison. This is not a "pretty picture" for lovers of independent and foreign films. And it represents a missed educational opportunity for adults and adolescents alike.

As the twentieth century unfolded, communities across the nation came to view education and schooling as synonymous. What went on within the school house walls, or "intentional learning," was considered education. The many sources of information people of all ages encountered from television, radio, magazines, newspapers, and movies was something else, but seldom referred to as education. This erroneous perception tends to keep communities from making the most of "incidental learning" opportunities.

The Internet, of course, has dramatically altered the media environment, but as with television, it is spewing forth a glut of information that, in the words of media critic Neil Postman, "rejects the necessity of interconnectedness, proceeds without context, argues for instancy against historical continuity, and offers fascination in place of complexity and coherence." This refuse of inert data and facts is rarely analyzed, applied, and evaluated, which is to say, not transformed to knowledge. As Postman and others argue, "modern man" in Western society is awash in information that is a form of garbage not only incapable of answering the most fundamental human questions but barely useful in providing coherent direction to the solution of even mundane problems.

As a result, young people are left with the impoverished notion that excellence is defined by achievement tests, and schools exist to provide them with information and skills necessary to obtain high-paying jobs. In this environment, education is reduced to economic utility, and lucrative employment exists to acquire consumer stuff. One result of this dysfunctional association between schooling and the economy is an overextended, debt-ridden, acquisitive populace. As we should learn from schooling, a good education, among others things, frees one from the "bondage of materialism."

In modern America, when we lament the passing of small retail stores sent to their demise by big box chains, we ought to include the local picture house. If the marketplace in our capitalist society won't support a small independent movie theater in towns, such as Elkhorn, and provide learning opportunities through film viewing and discussion groups, the public sector ought to. What is to prevent, local government and civic organizations from operating small theaters, such as the Sprague, selecting films for their educational value, and making them central to civic life? And what a productive way to spend Sunday afternoons!

The primary impediment to indigenous learning, for people of all ages, is imagination and public resources. In our society, we are easily blinded by a market mentality that limits perceptions. By educational, I'm referring to films that address the root meaning of the term, as in *education—to lead out or draw forth*" from its Latin root "e" (out of) and "duco" (to lead).

Embedded in this definition are learning experiences that open the mind, introduce ideas, and expand one's vision. This could help people of any age confront life's existential questions: Who are you? Where are you going? How will you get there? Such is a condition of an educative society, and an educative society is imperative for democracy to flourish. Otherwise, the people remain "subjects" rather than "citizens." This enterprising economic activity may not add much to the ledgers of "private wealth," but it would enhance our town and nation's "common wealth"

During the summers of 1955 and 1956 Dick Van learned valuable lessons on business and wealth. His summer employment involved working a small drive-in restaurant at the crossroads of highways 12 and 15 four miles north of town. Gordon Kennedy and Darrell Wales owned the short-order establishment along with The Traveler restaurant across the highway. Van's shifts, seven days a week, seven hours a day, coincided with those of Darrell's, from whom he received a short course in applied economics.

Among other things, Wales taught him the price of owning and operating an automobile and why he didn't need one then at the cost of being cash poor. On one occasion, when the kid no doubt was impertinent, Darrell left him with words carried through life, "The customer is always right." These days this concept is blown up and turned into a management course under the name "customer-focus" marketing. Darrell helped the boy understand that courtesy, consideration, and diplomacy goes a long way in life and is good for business. The good man passed away in the summer of 2009 after successfully operating restaurants in Elkhorn for over a half century.

One regret working summers at the drive-in was missing several booster Gray baseball games. Given the seven-day a week work schedule, Van managed to play only eight of the 13 games on the Grays' schedule in the summer of 1956. He carried a .423 average just .002 higher than Sonny Colombe, who hit .421. Sonny, a dependable shortstop, played all 13 games and deserved the title that season.

On several occasions, Van's mother drove to retrieve him from work, then sped back to the baseball diamond, so that the outfielder might catch the first inning. On one occasion, while undressed in the backseat attempting to put on his uniform, Helen Van tried to pass on the treacherous two-lane Highway 12 with a semi-truck bearing down. Fortunately, she made it around the slower car but not without the benign cooperation of both the oncoming truck and other auto driver. Given her adventures on the roadways, it is fortunate most of her driving was restricted to in town at slow speeds.

Earnings that summer, calculated at $1/hour, 49 hours a week, for 12 weeks, plus a few weekends into the fall, netted about $700 that had to last the entire school year. This income was augmented with earnings from cleaning the *Independent* newspaper office every Saturday morning. EHS girls were "low maintenance," but Van, as with other boys, needed money for dating and a fashionable wardrobe. EHS had several impeccably dressed teachers, particularly Arlene Zaffrann, Carol Bartingale, and Sam Kaplan, who set standards for all. The same can't be said, however, of Coach Suchy, who was directed by Superintendent Clarence Schacht to dress more appropriately than in t-shirt attire, when he emerged from the locker room.

11 **Girls**

The object of education is to prepare the young to
educate themselves throughout their lives.
Robert Maynard Hutchins,
President, University of Chicago

"**S**he chased him, until he caught her," Jon Dahle explained to a fellow teacher in the hallway outside his classroom. This was 1954, Dick Van's sophomore year, and Mr. Dahle was referring to classmate Patsy Tripp. "Pat" too was a sophomore and farm girl who had entered the Elkhorn schools the previous year as a freshman. She was the young boy's first love, and he was hers.

Pat, as with many fellow rural students, had a highly developed work ethic, and the two kids shared several classes that year—Latin, English, biology, and algebra. Yet, the fondest memories took place at the ballgames, "sock hops," and other school events. After home basketball contests, the two 15-year-olds walked to Dick Van's home, where his father would drive the 10-mile journey to her house in the Millard area of Sugar Creek Township.

It was a circuitous route, with embraces and sweet kisses exchanged, through a wooded area that turned the three-block trip into 30 minutes or more. It didn't matter how cold or snowy the winter night, this was the warmest excursion yet in their travel through youth. She from a family of four girls, and he of one with all boys would provide each other valuable interpersonal lessons during a wonderful time together.

Aside from being an athletically attractive girl, Pat was a superb student and the first in her family to attend college. This characteristic she shared with other young women—and men at EHS. There is something about humble backgrounds, strong work ethic, and academic excellence that go together. She was not alone as a high-achieving girl among the class of '57. Diane Babcock, who taught Dick Van to tie his shoes in kindergarten, was another and eventually married Sonny Colombe, quarterback and shortstop from the class of '56.

In fifth grade, when the gender gap is still minimal, classmates arranged for a match race between the fastest girl, Gail Pett, and the swiftest boy. The playground of the historic 1887 school was rain-soaked that day when the two runners turned at the designated tree midway through the race; Gail lost traction falling into a mud puddle. Unlike the great filly Ruffian, who shattered her leg in a 1975 match race, Gail did not have to be euthanized. She just trotted two blocks home for a change of clothing. Yet, it must be said that Dick Van occasionally has lived up to the name of the colt in that fateful race—Foolish Pleasure.

Phyllis Kexel, another popular and able student, participated in multiple school activities along with cheerleading. When senior classmates named the top girl and boy in various school culture categories, Phyllis and Van were labeled "most versatile." Elaine Johnson, a farm girl, graceful and lovely in an understated way, came to read every passage of this manuscript and offer valuable editing advice. After high school, Elaine married classmate Larry Yanke, a young man of wit and playful intellectual qualities. He was that lone 8th grader who voted for Adlai Stevenson in the mock 1952 Presidential election.

A regret the Van boys heard regularly from their mother was not having a daughter among her five births. She even had feminine names selected for the second wave: "Karen," "Judy," and "Linda" in that order. At one time, Dick and Roger simultaneously were dating classmates Karen and Judy Wenger, which prompted the boys to exclaim to their mother: "This is the closest you will get to girls named Karen and Judy, so "back off!"

Pat Tripp eventually married Jim Froehlke, class of '55, and earned a teaching degree. Jim was the brother of Helen, another popular classmate, who contributed to the school culture through class plays, yearbook staff, and as Prom Queen. Van and Helen dated some during their senior year, but more significantly, she was the cute 6th grader, from whom the kid received a sweet 11-year-old kiss, when he delivered a May Day basket to her home at Lake Wandawega on a beautiful spring day in 1951.

Pat and young Van's birthdays were two days apart —September 4th and 2nd respectively. At age 36 and the mother of four, she died of a brain tumor. A similar affliction had taken the life of one of her daughters two years earlier. As the song goes, sometimes, "the good die young," but one's first love is cherished forever.

12 **1957**

The historian is a prophet looking backwards.
Author Friedrich von Schlegel

It was a grand year for the Chevy Bel Air Sports Sedan and tail fins in general. Car styles during the carefree affluence of the decade reached its peak in 1957. It also was a great time for professional baseball in Wisconsin. The Braves a few years earlier had moved its hapless Boston franchise to Milwaukee, and the people of Wisconsin fell in love with their team. It helped that overnight the Braves were transformed into a National League contender, as young, budding stars came together. Most notable were Warren Spahn, who had become the game's finest left-handed pitcher, and Eddie Mathews, a handsome slugger who could light up the stadium with magnificent home runs. The best was saved for an unassuming young black outfielder from the South with a magical swing. Hank Aaron and a supporting cast of hard hitting and flame throwing mates would bring Milwaukee a World Series championship in 1957.

In Walworth County, EHS ball players were preparing again for a four-sport school year that tended to frustrate fellow Southern Lakes coaches and athletes. Why does

Elkhorn High, they asked, allow athletes to compete in two spring sports? The answer was simple—because they could! Soon others realized that it didn't make much difference, if they permitted boys to participate in baseball as well as track and field. Few excelled at both, and none in the Southern Lakes could compete at the level of Riese and the Van Scotter brothers, with the exception of several Wilmot athletes, who also played two spring sports.

The Elkhorn speedsters were looking forward to a new track season in the spring of '57 with their now veteran runners. But first, there would be a wonderful crisp autumn with footballs flying through the air, followed by the obligatory snowy, cold Wisconsin winter where hoopsters hoped to heat up the Kinne Gym. When gridiron hopefuls began practice in late summer, the county fair was underway adjacent to the football field. Early wind sprints again showcased the speed of Roger Van, Dick Van, and Bill Riese, but this fall the quick junior was putting even more distance between himself and his two senior teammates. When questioned by Coach Suchy to explain the gap, Dick Van responded that "he trained all summer just to maintain speed, while his brother sat around getting faster." This was not hyperbole.

Often the Wisconsin football season brings cold, rainy weather, but the fall of 1956 witnessed magnificent brisk game nights and weekends. Bill Riese broke a collarbone midway through the season, and Dick Van was slowed for several games with a nagging injury, but Roger Van lit up the scoreboard, and the Elks savaged a .500 season in the final game against Lake Geneva. The Resorters maintained control through three quarters behind the running of all-conference halfback, Larry Margraf, a 5'8," 180 lb. stout kid who ran like a snarly bobcat. Early in the fourth quarter, Dick Van gathered in a punt and handed the ball on a crossing pattern to his younger brother who, with the help of crisp blocks from Dave Fink and Jim Wuttke, scampered 50 yards for the winning score.

Dick Van's injury occurred in the first game as he popped through the line of scrimmage with a clear field ahead. There, he was "horse collared" and spun to the ground by a Milton linebacker, which would have earned him a 15-yard penalty in a few years. That "malicious" player was Jerry Chase who would be Van's teammate at Beloit College, where the two became best friends. Jerry was a wonderful example of an intelligent, small-town working class kid (his father operated an auto repair shop) that given a chance could excel. He was Phi Beta Kappa at Beloit and went to Stanford University for a Ph.D. in mathematics. The guy was brilliant and a durable, smart defensive back.

Basketball was much the same as the Elks finished in the middle of the conference but dazzled spectators and opponents alike with their quickness up and down the floor. At 6'0" Dan Morrow and Jon Platts were the tallest players, while Jim Mason and Dick Van, both 5'10", and Roger Van at 5'9" handled backcourt chores. Although small in stature, the pint-sized quintet made every game thrilling. The year's highlight was a mid-season upset of conference champ Burlington, with a frontline of 6'8" George Vorpagel flanked by two 6'3" forwards.

The Elks sagging zone kept "big George" in check, while its fast-break offense was effective enough. On defense, Suchy had Dick Van pick up the ball handler at mid-court. When he passed to the flank, Van's responsibility was to drop off in front of Vorpagel and keep him from the ball. This worked. As the buzzer ending the game sounded, Dick Van was fouled and sent to the free throw line. The outcome was not in doubt, and players had departed for their respected locker rooms, but Burlington fans gathered along the end line to rattle the normally unflappable shooter. Among those dressed in "Demon orange and black" was the opponent's distracting cheerleader, Joanie Moore, who at the time was dating the Elkhorn kid in satin shorts. "Over the rim and in" Van repeated to himself, as he scored the game's final two points in a 55 to 49 victory.

The Burlington contest was atypically low-scoring for the "race horse Elk five" that averaged 67 points per game that season. Both zone defenses were stingy even though the teams shot at a 50 percent clip. Yet, typical for the Elks on this night was their offensive balance: Dick Van (14), Platts (13), Roger Van (12), and Morrow (10) all were in double figures, while towering all-conference center Vorpagel was held to 14 points. For the season, all five of the EHS starters averaged over 10 points per game.

The next night Elkhorn travelled to Delavan for a rare Saturday game just before the winter holiday break. For three quarters, a tenacious press kept the favored Elks in check. The Comets seemed particularly spunky making effective use of the school's antiquated "bandbox" gym. Their backcourt of Dave Porter, Mike Skopec, and Jim Jonuska forced more turnovers than the sure-handed Elks were accustomed to giving up.

The Elks seemed to be feeling fatigue from the Burlington game in which the starting five played the entire game. Tonight, Suchy would employ his bench, but this was slim with only Bill Riese and two sophomores, Don Koepnick and Bill Lock in reserve. Lock and Koepnick would help lead the Elks to conference titles the following two years, but they had only been on the varsity for a few weeks. Early on Suchy had three "tall" upperclassmen in reserve that turned in their uniforms after riding the bench. So, the coach was prepared to ride his "Pony Express" as long as possible.

As the fourth quarter opened, the Elks were down five points when their endurance took hold with several steals and fast breaks. Midway through the quarter, Delavan's top scorer, Frank McClellan, left the game with five fouls, and the Comets lost their force. Elkhorn outscored them by 15 points in the final quarter and pulled away to a 69-59 victory. McClellan was a talented 6'3" kid with big, strong hands that reflected his years milking cows on the family dairy farm. Yet, he had a jump shot that was as soft and sweet as Marilyn Monroe's smile. The next year, Dick Van and McClellan would be roommates as freshmen at Beloit College and remain life-long friends. The same was true for Skopec and Roger Van who attended Marquette University together and maintained a friendship in Southern California, where Mike is a psychiatrist and Van a periodontist. And the coach of that Delavan team was the former EHS star, Don Breidenbach.

A few weeks later, the Elks traveled to Lake Geneva where they were challenged by another peculiar venue. The school theater doubled as a hard court, and players, the basketball type, occasionally ran off the stage in pursuit of the ball. Game pace was fast, and the team dressed in deep red and gold uniforms, led by sharp shooting guards Dick Burnett and Larry Margraf, outgunned the purple and gold 91 to 85.

Earlier that week, the Elks traveled across the border to take on Hebron in a similar theatrical setting. The Green Giants, playing with younger relatives from its 1952 Illinois state championship team, tallied 95 points. Coach Suchy sardonically commented on the Elks' tenacious defense.

By 1957, the boys had become resourceful in overcoming "Sunday afternoon" doldrums. Using a bogus excuse, Dick Van borrowed Coach Suchy's keys to the school, where upon he relayed them to Jon Platts who high tailed it to the family Hardware Store downtown and copied the master. There after, the ballplayers could escape to the Kinne Gym on Sunday afternoons and hone their basketball skills outside the notice of both school officials and WIAA regulators, who closely monitored the quantity of school practice sessions.

13 Fast Times at Elkhorn High

*We are only alive in those moments
when our hearts are conscious of our treasurers.*
Thornton Wilder, author

The uniforms changed for the 1957 track season, but still represented the wrong sport. Now runners donned purple basketball jerseys that a decade earlier served the junior high "Pioneer" teams. At least they were lighter with only the letters "Elkhorn" across the front giving the appearance of a track singlet. And they matched the purple gym shorts. If a kid today were handed such a shabby uniform on joining the team, he or she likely would turn it in and resign.

The lack of fashion, however, didn't slow down the Elk thinclads in 1957. This year for the first time, they would enter the state's mythical indoor championship, the Madison West Relays, held at the University of Wisconsin's indoor track facility. Junior, Roger Van, dispelled a silly myth by demonstrating that he was quick out of the blocks in equaling the meet 60-yard dash record and beating Menasha's Hyde. Later in the day, the Elks 880-yard relay team (with sophomore

Ron Pearsall replacing Ward) established a new meet record in this event. Earlier, the sprint medley foursome finished fourth with half-miler Don Kayser running anchor. Riese, Pearsall, and Dick Van ran the other three legs.

For their efforts, the Elks finished third in the Class B division just off the pace of Kohler (as in the plumbing company) and Port Washington, a perennial hotbed of track talent, 30 minutes north of Milwaukee on Lake Michigan.

The outdoor season would be more of the same, as the Elks relay team sailed through dual meets undefeated. In addition to running the sprints, Bill Riese exceeded Bill Ward's shot put mark. A few years later, the youngest Van, Alan, another dash man would toss the shot put and discus even farther. These guys were athletes first with track and field falling somewhat in the mix of multiple sports.

It was beautiful weather that spring, and Roger Van kept sports writers following his progress as he lowered the school 220-yard mark from 22.0 flat to 21.7 and then 21.1. The times were at home meets on the County Fairgrounds straightway, so they would not be an official record by state standards. Still, adjusted for the track and non-curve, his projected time for the furlong would have been about 21.5, below the 22.0 all-time state mark for the event. He also lowered his 100-yard best to 10 seconds flat.

The weather remained spectacular until the eve of the State Finals in Madison as storm clouds gathered in the late May atmosphere. The trackmen woke to a gloomy Saturday before making the trek to Madison that morning. On his walk to the high school, Dick Van stopped downtown at the Rexall drugstore to buy the *Madison Capital Times*. His first glance was at the weather page, and the report wasn't pretty. Only after this did he check the sports page and list of qualifiers for the state meet.

Conditions grew worse as the team arrived at the stadium in Madison. This was most unlike the pleasant climate a year earlier. Roger Van was hustled over to the University indoor track adjacent to Camp Randall because the outdoor facilities were unfit for field competition. Runners preparing for trial heats that morning had to warm up indoors near the basketball court. The younger Van also competed in the broad jump, an event in which he would take second place, in a highly competitive contest, to Greendale's Jerry Casey.

Soon the outdoor races began under a steady, cold rain. The visibility was so impaired that runners, peering down the track at the start of the sprints and hurdles, could not see the finish line. To prevent a mishap, the older Van steadied the starting blocks for his younger brother, who swooshed to a comfortable victory in the 100-yard prelims.

Riese and Dick Van would run in the 220 yard event. Coach Hennum, on the advice of Suchy, had the two seniors reverse races with Roger Van for the sectional qualifying meet in Fort Atkinson a week earlier. Roger was the defending 220-yard champion and his 21.1 seconds was the state's all-time fastest for the event. As Suchy reasoned, competitors would avoid the 220 and stack up in the 100-yard event.

He was right: Hyde, living up to his name, switched to 180-yard low hurdles, which he ran along with the 100-yard dash. Menasha was forgoing points in the 880-yard relay, in hopes of Hyde scoring big as a double winner in individual events. Most other top Class B sprinters, given the choice, also selected what they thought would be the less competitive of the two sprint races. They also were right; the eventual winner in the 220, Charles

Holmes of Portage, located in the central part of the state, finished 5th in the 100-yard dash.

Roger Van played his part in this scenario by racing to victory in the finals of the 100-yard dash early that afternoon. On a soggy track, he legged 10.2 seconds, ahead of Menasha's Hyde, as well as the Class A (10.5) and Class C (10.7) winners. This was no day for fast times, but had the weather been suitable, the speedster would have run at least 9.9 on dry cinders.

When Dick Van entered the track for his heat of the 220-yard dash, he was greeted by a huge "puddle" at the most inappropriate spot, precisely where his starting blocks were to be placed. "Nature's god" was not looking kindly on him, as his lane was the only one with a "water hole," the size of Lake Como. Van couldn't avoid the wetness this time. He had run fast races that spring and triumphed at both the Southern Lakes Conference and qualifying sectional meets, but this was not his day. Bill Riese didn't fare much better in his heat, and the Elks would not have a runner in the finals of the 220-yard dash. As Microsoft founder Bill Gates remarked, "Success is a lousy teacher, it seduces people into thinking they can't lose."

Elkhorn had picked up one point in the 880-yard run through the effort of Kayser. What made the 220-yard elimination more painful was the eventual 4th place finish of Robert Vick, a Hartford runner, whom Dick Van had outrun that spring in the Whitewater Relays. Vick was not a gracious "spoiler," so it appeared, or maybe it was just his ill-timed attempt at humor. In retrospect, this race was an immense disappointment in which "matter triumphed over mind." Still, it was a lesson learned that would serve him well in future contests.

The 800-yard relay was still to come, a race the foursome anticipated with confidence. The Elk relay team had been undefeated throughout the season, including its winning performance at the indoor Madison West Relays. Menasha would not be a contender this year, but Sturgeon Bay was entered and had the state's best Class B time along with Elkhorn. Making this match-up all the more interesting was that Sturgeon Bay, an apple orchard paradise located in Door County, was the hometown of Fred Suchy.

Coach Suchy had been a local multi-sport star with close ties still to the area. Each fall, Suchy would bring back to Elkhorn bushels of apples in his pick-up truck where his ballplayers feasted on the nutritious fruit for several weeks.

At the Van Scotter home, when the contents of a bushel neared the bottom, and some apples were inevitably mushy, the Van boys would test their skill at "avoiding the flying fruit." As one brother remained on the back porch with a soft apple in hand, preparing to throw it at his sibling, the other would run a zigzag pattern toward a neighboring yard. This was great fun that tested both the boys' throwing accuracy and "broken field" running.

Unfortunately, the two teams did not run "head-to-head" in this last event of the day. Sturgeon Bay would be in Heat 1 of three and Elkhorn in the final one. The rains finally were letting up as the Clippers set sail in their heat, recording a time slower than desired. A few minutes later, the skies parted, the sun peeped through, and the "god of Nike" shined down on the Elks who ran to a mud-splattered victory in the event.

When meet points were tallied, Elkhorn had earned the 2nd place trophy losing only to Platteville, a city located in the southwestern region of the state, by one point—21 to 20. Had the elder Van outrun Hartford's Vick on this day and taken 4th place, thereby adding two points, his team would have taken home the big trophy in 1957. Runner up was nice, and the trophy case back home had one more award, but the disappointment would be etched in his memory.

14 **Purple Golden Year**

Blessed are the meek, for they shall inherit the earth.
Jesus' Sermon on the Mount

In the fall of 1957, Bill Riese would head to college at Platteville State (now the University of Wisconsin–Platteville) but only for one year. He would remain in Elkhorn working four decades as an operating engineer, driving a road grader.

Earlier that spring, Frank Eames, a member of the 1946 Elks champion football team, contacted Perry MaGill, co-owner of a suburban Chicago steel company. Eames had joined his father Claude "Mud" Eames at the *Elkhorn Independent*, the venerable weekly that his family owned and operated for three generations. Perry, the Van boys' uncle, and Frank were graduates of Beloit College. Eames recommended that MaGill, also the colleges' alumni fund drive chair that year, pave the way for Dick Van to attend Beloit. MaGill agreed, and Eames drove the boy to campus the week of the state meet where, among other things, he introduced Van to the Beloit track coach. The small Midwest Ivy college and the nascent scholar athlete would be a perfect fit for the next four years.

Relay members Roger Van and Ron Pearsall would lead the Elk football team that fall and be two members of the fastest backfield in the state. The other half of the backfield-relay team was quarterback Jon Platts and halfback Gary Ellsworth. These were not heavyweights: Pearsall was the "big man" at 175 lbs, while Platts and Ellsworth weighed in at 160 and Van Scotter 145. But it was the highest scoring team in EHS history and most exciting.

Roger Van scored a league leading 91 points that included 15 touchdowns in eight games while averaging 8.1 yards per carry. Four of those scores were dramatic kick returns, while he also led the team in pass receptions with 16 catches for 374 yards—23.4 yards per catch. By mid-season, opponents aimed punts toward the sidelines and kick offs to anyone else on the field, in an attempt to eliminate devastating returns. This prescription apparently was overlooked for the final game at Lake Geneva. Van promptly gathered in the opening kick off and returned it 85 yards for a touchdown. As one Southern Lakes coach jokingly instructed his players, "If in doubt, head to the end zone and tackle him when he gets there." For this, the speedster was named the co-Southern Lakes most valuable player and to the all-state team.

Jim Wuttke and Van are two of the best to ever play their respective positions at EHS, based on data compiled by long-time coach, Dean Wilson. Wuttke, a devastating blocker, still ranks number one in tackles for a season with 141, which he did in only eight games. Van, likewise, is the top punt returner in school history with a season high three touchdowns and 298 yards for a 27.1 average His career, five kick returns for touchdowns and pass reception average also are tops. Toss in over 1,500 career rushing yards, and he is the number one all around back in school history.

This was the beginning of a grand year for the "purple and gold." Platts and Van Scotter, along with juniors, Koepnick, Lock, and Tom Wescott would lead the team to a conference basketball title during the winter and nearly claim the regional title. Coach Suchy's squad fell in a close match to formidable Kenosha but came back to stop Beloit for the regional consolation title. In doing so, the 1957-58 Elks destroyed the myth that the Southern Lakes couldn't compete with the best of the Big Eight.

Yet, the '58 class saved their best for the track season. Two years earlier, the Elk thinclads were neophytes in Madison, and a year before they missed the state crown by an eyelash—or a puddle. Again, the uniforms changed, to gold basketball shirts with purple numbers: In three track seasons, only the color of the singlet differed—from white to purple to gold—but not the sport. The boys never seemed to notice—or at least not care.

The irony here is that the youngsters in the '50s dressed with care, even immaculately, for school and social events, while their athletic uniforms reflected the frugality of the era. Several decades later, American youth would respond to their perceived opulence by dressing in "thrift-shop grunge," but, in other ways, expect a life of abundance.

Many boys, in the 50s, made an annual pre-school trip to downtown Milwaukee and Johnny Walker's Clothing to the chagrin of Elkhorn merchants. George Cain and Howard Dailey, the town's reigning shopkeepers, attempted to attract young natty dressers, but it was a tall order stocking stylish charcoal grey suits, melon and chartreuse sweaters, bright dress shirts, and black slacks with pink strips. Johnny Walker's still is thriving on Wisconsin Avenue near the Milwaukee River

Bridge, with a fine line of zoot suits. Only the clientele has changed to metro African-Americans. It wasn't much of a leap from the wardrobes of Sonny Colombe, Jack Kirkham, Jon Platts, and Roger Van to its current customers.

Adults also showed respect for institutions and occasions through dress and decorum in early decades. Top hats for men were particularly stylish, and women topped off wardrobes with a fashionable bonnet, fastened with a hairpin. Fred MaGill and Henry Van were men who got dirt under their finger nails and used coarse soaps to scrub after a hard day's work. When they donned bib overalls each work day, this was not a fashion statement, as some attempt nowadays.

Come weekends, Dad took pride in wearing a pair of gabardines and dress shirt, and one rarely sees a photo of grandpa not in a fine suit of clothes. Henry's wardrobe for Sundays and special occasions included several suits, complements of Cain Clothing Store. Neighbor George "Shorty" Cain at a svelte, 5'5" tall, was the same size as Van. Shorty wore a suit daily for work; after a year or so, he would pass the "threads" on to Dad, who, despite his blue-collar status, was among the best dressed men in town.

From 1956 to 1958, during this golden period, the federal government ran a budget surplus, foreign trade balances were positive, economic growth on the rise, home building at record levels, consumer savings high, and household debt low. Yet, Dick Van thought he was well-heeled as he departed for college in the fall of 1957 with two modest suitcases, a typewriter, and AM radio.

A half century later, the opposite holds: government is running huge annual deficits, the federal debt burgeons, the foreign trade deficit is growing, business productivity sluggish, unemployment up, consumers floating in debt with income disparity increasing and homes in foreclosure, while kids feel entitled to live like the "profligate son."

In 1956, during the Eisenhower Administration, Congress passed the Interstate Highway Act that led to over 40,000 miles of new construction including elaborate beltways around major cites connecting them to local roads. Today the nation's physical infrastructure is in decay with roads, bridges, sewers, electrical grids, schools, airports, and mass transit overburdened, outdated, and in disrepair. Something happened!

15 Corrupting Affluence

The paradox of our time is that we have taller buildings but shorter tempers, bigger houses but smaller families, wider freeways but narrower viewpoints. We buy more, but enjoy less.
George Carlin

What happened was that the economy was transforming from a nation of producers to a land of consumers. Americans began living better after a couple decades of scarcity during the Great Depression and World War II. By the 1950s, the U.S. economy was running in high gear as the world's leading manufacturer with more and new goods coming off assembly lines. To keep this economic growth going, consumer demand was revved up through extensive marketing efforts and an expanding range of credit measures, particularly the plastic card, open to abuse in the hands of extreme buyers and predatory lenders.

For all its assumed simplicity and innocence, the 1950s was the beginning of the United States' consumption binge. Many desired to own bigger, powerful "muscle" cars; move to the suburbs with larger homes and spacious lawns; and acquire the many new home appliances displayed in stores of shopping malls—

all indicators of the nation's growing prosperity. "Since Ronald Reagan's presidency," *Newsweek* editor Fareed Zakaria reminds us, "Americans have consumed more than we produced and have made up the difference by borrowing." In effect, we have been "eating our seed corn."

Harvard economist, John Kenneth Galbraith, described this emergence of material comforts and changing national mindset in his 1958 classic *The Affluent Society*. Another influential work that tapped into the pulse of the decade was William Whyte's study of American corporate life described in *The Organization Man* (1956). Whyte, a Princeton educated sociologist and journalist, worked for *Fortune* when he conducted extensive interviews with CEOs of corporations, including General Electric and Ford.

America was changing; we were on the "cutting edge" of a huge cultural transformation with little clue of what was swirling around us. Even Galbraith and Whyte, writing in the mid-1950s, couldn't understand the seismic change in American culture that would unfold. Consumption was throwing off the chains of the old production-oriented society and allowing people to buy into fantasy, writes film critic Neal Gabler. Consumption, teaming with its hedonistic accomplice "entertainment" provides the same intoxication: "the sheer endless pleasure of emancipation from reason, from responsibility, from tradition, from class, and from the other bonds that restrained the self."

Starting in the Fifties, most Americans expected more—more extravagant automobiles, appliances, homes, and televisions. In time, the personal computer and video technology expanded our desires, followed by the Internet, cell phones, digital cameras, compact disc, iPods, and Blackberries. Much of this is devoted to marketing products. We had come to live in a high-tech, instant communications age, offering consumers a wide range of designer goods fueled by expanding debt. New buying habits of a high-consumption economy were eroding the "Protestant ethic" and "Puritan temper."

The tragedy in this scenario begins in the 1950s, as people bought into the myth of "American Dream" that "Madison Avenue" relentlessly marketed. By the early 1970s, this myth was fading: even though industrial productivity increased, wages stagnated as workers lost bargaining power. By now they were "hooked," as many attempted to maintain the "dream" by acquiring debt in increasingly multiple forms "pushed" by financial institutions as well as manufacturers and retailers. Families also turned to two wage earners, which took its toll on domestic life.

Today's youth are children of the "boomers," who born after 1946 never knew the deprivation of the Great Depression and the sacrifice of World War II. Most grew up with a sense of entitlement then attempted to pass material comfort on to their children. Unfolding around them was a corporate, suburban, institutional environment that left many with a cultural barrenness and insatiable desires. This doesn't work, and "burnout," a socio-psychological concept, emerged. Burnout is not a result of overwork, as conventionally thought, but of boredom. As George Carlin suggested, "We have multiplied our possessions, but reduced our values." The emptiness of materialism takes a toll.

A salient inquiry of philosophers, over the ages, has been the nature of happiness. Happiness is the purpose for living and the essence of a good life, but even Thomas Jefferson explained in the *Declaration of Independence* that we only have an "inalienable right" to the "*pursuit* of happiness." It must be earned and is not obtained through pleasure and multiple possessions. Rather the temple of happiness, we learn from philosophy, is entered through the courtyard of simplicity, restraint, and service.

One bit of family history held in memory is our humble backgrounds. The house on Washington Street, a block north of downtown, was modest by any definition. The Van brothers shared a small bedroom with twin beds, simple desk, and small closet. But then we didn't have a large wardrobe, and the dining room table was sufficient for study in the evenings. No blaring television set existed to interrupt learning. No iPod with phone jack planted in the ear would break one's concentration.

The only communications that might be perceived as blaring in the 1950s were radio broadcasts of baseball games on Sunday afternoons over the "backyard fence." As the Van brothers played catch, they could hear the Chicago White Sox game coming from Lawrence "Toad" Hutton's house, as he worked the family garden. From another angle, George "Shorty" Cain tuned in Earl Gillespie and the Braves' play-by-play on Milwaukee's WTMJ. Positioned strategically in their backyard, the Van boys also could hear the Cubs from WGN Chicago and enjoy a symphony of baseball sounds.

Elkhorn did have its upscale houses, early-twentieth century style, but these mostly were in a neighborhood just south and west of downtown where many city "power brokers" resided. Washington Street had its share of notable homes with classic front porches, but generally the housing mix reflected the equalitarian nature of the community. Lawyers, doctors, and entrepreneurs lived in proximity to insurance agents, realtors, and store owners, who resided among tradesmen and factory workers. We all were in it together, and this heterogeneity was mirrored in the public schools.

Still, it was the sons and daughters of doctors, lawyers, and executives who attended "Midwest Ivy" colleges such as Alverno, Carleton, and Lawrence. Only through "divine economic intervention" was Dick Van able to enroll at Beloit. Many of his mates from working-class families headed for nearby Whitewater State, if they attended college at all.

Few families benefited more from public education, i.e., "government schools," than the Van Scotters. In conservative Walworth County, it was commonplace to complain of taxes and decry government. Yet, it was public fire departments that our grandfathers and fathers proudly served; the sheriff's department that captured the Touhy gang; city workers that strung decorations each holiday season; the sanitation department that gathered liquor bottles weekly; and schools that, while educating children, served as the village's entertainment centerpiece. In addition, state agricultural extension programs and research aided local farmers, while federal price support kept revenues stable. Residents also have enjoyed the county and state's park system. Many EHS grads attended college with financial aid from the GI Bill, while seniors enjoy retirement aided by Medicare and Social Security. Indeed, government and "socialism" has been good for the citizens of this proud, independent town.

The term is misunderstood, misused, and abused by many Americans to the point that sensible social and economic policy, such as omnipresent medical care, is resisted. In a practical sense, socialism is simply *a belief in the ability of people to work together to solve problems.* Isn't this what a good community and team do? Doesn't this principle also apply to capitalism, when firms are ethical, collaborative, and patient? While capitalism is grounded in private ownership, socialism is based on common ownership. Both are necessary in modern economic society.

Free markets in themselves are insufficient for a good society. While they can produce people's *wants* efficiently, they fall short in addressing people's *needs,* such as universal access to education and healthcare. Private markets also stumble in providing what we use in common, e.g., police and fire protections, roads and mass transit. It is these "market imperfections" that are incompatible with fundamental democratic requirements: balancing freedom with equality and private wealth with common wealth.

From another perspective, reports *The Atlantic Monthly*, the number of American corporate and business assets recently nationalized is $82.3 billion. This sounds like a lot, but when compared to assets held privately, $39.2 trillion, it amounts to just .21 percent.

It's easy to take our affluence for granted and believe that we've done it all by ourselves. The novelist Saul Bellow called this a "lonely arrogance" that says "I should be self-sufficient." As if, I've earned everything that ever came to me. Deep down, we probably know how untrue this is and feel great doubt. The cure for such egotism is to accept that we all are part of a larger whole and have arrived at where we are today "on the backs of those who came before us." The flip side of this paradox is that we are all pilgrims, guests, and vulnerable. As Benjamin Franklin remarked on the eve of Revolution, "We can either hang together or hang separately." In the words of novelist Christopher Morley, "Life is a foreign language that most people mispronounce."

Unless we get our economic house in order, this sequence will reverse for our grandchildren and great grandchildren. If manufacturing continues to drift overseas to China, India, Mexico, and elsewhere, future generations of Americas will not even have decent industrial jobs. Aside from those who acquire careers in education, medicine, and technology, a growing number will be relegated to low-paying service work in "big box" retail stores, hotels, and other institutions. Without a vibrant, industrial, middle-class, even the incomes earned by physicians, dentists, lawyers, realtors, and many others will pale in comparison to what our generation earned.

In 1941, publishing magnate, Henry Luce, proclaimed in *Time* magazine that this was the American Century. The U.S. triumph in World War II, in concert with economic prosperity and political respectability of the 1950s, established U.S. supremacy. During that decade and the 1960s, our nation invested in the infrastructure of the middle class. We built schools for the "baby boomers," opened new campuses for public colleges and universities, expanded the state park system, widened old roads, and broadened library access.

Those of us growing up in the Fifties benefited immensely from government programs. The middle class and those who aspire to middle-class status need and value public services. The wealthy don't especially value these programs: they generally don't send their children to public schools, take books out of libraries, use public transportation, and spend time in parks. So they resist paying taxes to support this social infrastructure at the expense of a vibrant middle class and democracy.

The American Century vanished and was relatively short-lived as global events during the remaining decades of the century cast doubt over the muscularity of the United States' power. By the 1980s, in the aftermath of the Vietnam War and with oil shortages, random terrorist threats, and periodic economic recessions, Americans felt their power declining. Political leaders, for the most part, refused to acknowledge this decline, and no one bothered to tell the average family who struggle to "make ends meet."

The problems we face today are structural and bringing back the old America will be daunting. This is not the 1950s, when a farmer, small business, or would-be homeowner secured a loan from the State Bank or National Bank fronting Wisconsin Street with its impressive pillars. The bank officer might be someone you knew, may be a neighbor, who took an interest in your success and the security of its loans. Today that loan likely would be sold to a banker, broker, or speculator on Wall Street and end up in some far-flung financial market across the globe. Those who have taken hostage of our financial system, relates Chris Hedges in *Empire of Illusion: The End of Literacy and the Triumph of Spectacle* (2009), told us that the old means of making capital by producing and manufacturing are outdated. They assured us that "money could be made out of money." They insisted that financial markets could be self-regulating. Ours collapsed.

Through its influence over markets, the media, foreign policy, politics, Congress, and consumers, corporate power is immense, suggesting that our nation is more a plutocracy than democracy. When Republican Theodore Roosevelt arrived at the White House in 1901, he announced that his administration would reign in the nation's industrial giants, whom he called "malefactors of great wealth." What progress TR made in "trust busting" dissipated in the Twenties under feckless executives and Congress in Washington. During the 1930s, Democratic President Franklin Delano Roosevelt took on the corporate power of what he called "economic royalists." Two decades later, in his farewell speech, Republican Dwight D. Eisenhower warned of the "Military-Industrial Complex."

Concern over the anonymity of a corporate state, or what political philosopher Shelton S. Wolin labeled "inverted totalitarianism," has been bipartisan. So, however, have been the facilitators of corporate power in recent decades. Few political leaders have the courage to denounce this power for fear of being called "socialist", "communist", or strangely enough "liberal." To resist the growth of such economic hegemony is to take a "conservative" position and defend this nation's enduring principles—liberty, equality, and justice.

It has been said that "Our parents labored as farmers, mechanics, plumbers, and industrial workers so that we could become engineers, doctors, lawyers, architects, and teachers. In turn, we work so that our children might become poets, musicians, artists, philosophers, and theologians, who help shed light on the shadows of our lives."

Speaking of shadows, our nation is going through another periodic religious revival, where many call for the return of traditional values while desiring extravagant automobiles, spacious homes, and more electronic "toys." It's a hypocritical cry for divine awakening, while attempting to fill an empty spirit with more stuff. Few people thought to fill this void with convivial activities that require patience, courage, integrity, simplicity, and knowledge—all the stuff of character. Such behavior, not worshipping economic markets, is the true "conscience of a conservative."

16 **State Champions**

In 1958, again dressed in "thrift-store" uniforms, the Elkhorn track team won the Wisconsin Class B State Championship, establishing standards that would last for decades. Two years earlier, EHS was an intriguing newcomer on the track scene, and a year later the "almost team," but now they held the first and only state track title in school history.

None of this came as a surprise to track enthusiasts across the Badger state. Roger Van had been pulling EHS track out of infancy for three years. As long as there was a pair of "spikes" to be had in the athletic department closet, there was a kid who wanted to run, jump, and throw on the team. No NIKE shoe company existed then, nor were there overpriced Adidas, Puma, New Balance, Asics, Brooks, and Saucony treads to wear. The team only had "spot-built" spikes and thick-soled tennis shoes to cushion their steps.

The season got off to an inauspicious start with a third place finish at the indoor Madison West Relays. Roger Van repeated as 60-yard dash champ and again runner up in broad jump, but the 880-yard relay foursome came in third. The first two-legs of that team were new in opening for Pearsall and Roger Van. Gary Ellsworth and Jon Platts were not as quick out of the blocks and off the turns as Riese and Dick Van had been, so by the time Roger Van got the baton for the final leg he was in tight quarters. As Dolly Parton's daddy explained when she dressed in a small sweater: "You shouldn't try to put 50 pounds of potatoes in a 25-pound sack." The track was too crowded, and Van could never get free around the tight curves and bunched field.

In early May, Van ran 100 yards at the Fort Atkinson Invitation in 9.9 seconds, breaking the 10-second barrier. A week later, the Elks captured the Southern Lakes championship rolling up 79½ points; almost double that of runner up Mukwonago with 43 points. That weekend the Sentry food store in Elkhorn was giving away Eddie Fisher records, and teenagers were snapping them up. Van had captured the 100, 220, and broad jumps title while the 880 and sprint medley relay teams cruised to victory. A week later, the Elks won the sectional meet in Whitefish Bay, a suburban community on Milwaukee's north shore, qualifying in five individual events and two relays for the state meet to be held the following week.

It was a warm Saturday that greeted the high school athletes on May 30, 1958 at Ripon College, but the track and infield were soggy from rains the previous day. The University of Wisconsin had dug up its track at Camp Randall after the 1957 season in order to expand the stadium for football. While Class A teams were competing at Milwaukee North stadium, Class B and C athletes were in Ripon. In the 100-yard dash, Van established control of the race early and repeated his winning performance running 10.1.

Earlier that day in the broad jump, he staged a classic dual with his three-year rival Dick Fowler from Port Washington High. Off and on during the meet, Port and Elkhorn would alternate holding first place in the standings. During the prelims, Van took the lead with a jump of 21' 8", but Fowler responded in the finals with a leap of 22' 4". The event would come down to the final jump, and a muddy runway required Van to start on the grass, turning on to the runway just prior to the take-off board. Coach Marvin Fruth, who had taken over for Hennum, strategically inserted a piece of cardboard at the 22-foot mark as a guide and incentive. Van sprinted toward the sawdust pit and, saving his best for last, leaped 22' 9¼" breaking the state Class B record that had stood for 21 years.

Platts added two points to the Elks total by leaping 20'8" in the broad jump. Shortly, thereafter, the sprint medley team contributed four points with another fourth place finish. Junior, Bob Wolff ran the anchor half-miler leg, while Pearsall, Platts, and Don Riese, Bill's younger brother, brought the baton to him.

The last event of the day was the 880-yard relay, and a victory would ensure first place for Elkhorn in the meet. Port Washington, anticipating a showdown, saved their best runners for this relay, but with Van at the anchor, the Elks flew to victory with a record time of 1:32.7. Their 28 point total placed them on the victory platform along with Port Washington (24 points) and Hartford (20 points). With this, 1957-58 stands as arguably the finest year in Elkhorn sports history.

24. 1957 Track Team. Row 1: Roger Van Scotter, Cecil Belk, Don Riese, Gary Ellsworth, John Lauderdale, Grant Mulder, Gary Breidenbach, Joe Sorenson, manager. Row 2: Coach Marvin Fruth, Jim Boardman, Dave Purcell, Dick Van Scotter, Jon Platts, Lee Zanin, Dave Fink, Bill Riese, Ron Pearsall, coach Gordon Hennum

25. 1957 880-yard relay team: left to right, Bill Riese, Dick Van Scotter, Ron Pearsall, and Roger Van Scotter

26. Dick Van Jump Shooter 1956-57 season

27. 21.1 220-yard dash 1957

28. Tom Hyde (Menasha) and Roger Van after 100-yard
    dash finals 1957

29. Seniors Pat Tripp and Dan Morrow 1957

30. Most Versatile – Phyllis Kexel and Dick Van 1957

31. Lorraine Hotel downtown at Wisconsin and Walworth Streets, circa 1956

32. 1957 Yearbook Staff: Front row: Larry Birtzer, Leon Walter. Middle Row: Dick Van Scotter, Gail Pett, Diane Babcock, Pat Tripp. Top Row: Larry Yanke,

Barb Ellsworth, Larry Kolden, Helen Froehlke, Dave Fink, Lee Zanin, Bob Vermillon, Sandy Guif, and Elaine Johnson

33. Running back

34. 1957 Offense: Relay Team Back Field: Gary Ellsworth (32), Jon Platts (QB), Roger Van Scotter (15), Ron Pearsall (27). Front line: left to right, Bob Wolff, Bob Bulger, Don Riese, Larry Rouse, Jim Wuttke, Dave Purcell, Dave Nelson

35. Beloit College Record Setting 4x110, 4x220, 4x440-yard relay teams: left to right, Don Fisher (Milwaukee), Richard Van Scotter, Coach Carl Nelson, Jon Parvin (Port Edwards), and Harv Flodin (Oak Park, Illinois)

36. 1979 South Florida Running Team: left to right Bob
    Layton (Plantation), Bill Springer (Fort Lauderdale),
    Alberto Echeverria (Miami), and Richard Van Scotter
    (Boca Raton)

37. Orange Bowl 10K Coconut Grove in Miami 1980 – 32:50, top Florida masters' time

38. Oregon Hood-to-Coast Relay 1999 – Row 1: David Bowden (Fort Lauderdale), Bob Martin (Atlanta), Mike Skeels (Portland), Ron Kita (New Hampshire), Richard Van Scotter (Colorado), Mike Kaiel (Portland). Row 2: Greg Jacobs (Oregon), Bob Layton (Plantation), Victor Beltran (Boca Raton), Bill Spencer (New Hampshire), Bill Springer (Fort Lauderdale), George Baier (Portland)

39. State Champions 1958—left to right: Assistant coach

Neil Thieleke, Don Riese, Bob Wolff, Jon Platts, Ron Pearsall, Gary Ellsworth, Roger Van, head coach Marvin Fruth, Superintendent C.A. Schacht, Principal Jack Refling

17 Life After High School

In 1977, author Ralph Keyes explored people's high school experiences in his book *Is There Life after High School?* What he found, among celebrities, was that memories were a) enduring, b) pleasurable, and c) painful. Many of us might check (d) all of the above.

After years in education, some closely involved with schools, including co-founding one, I've come away with a sense that the hand dealt my family and peers at Elkhorn High was pretty good. For some, however, high school was a vast wasteland even humiliating experience. When asked what they liked best about high school, the answer might well be "nothing." A graduate school friend and educator once remarked that the zenith of the American high school came in 1969, after which the learning environment, corrupted by the larger culture, drifted downward, leveling off at times but never reaching the high point of earlier decades. She makes a sound observation.

James Conant, former president of Harvard University and Ambassador to West Germany, headed a study of the American High School in the late 1950s and published its results in a succinct but widely read 1959 book. Conant observed that many of our nation's "best and brightest" students were not sufficiently challenged in their studies and that small schools were unable to offer a comprehensive and rigorous academic curriculum.

What followed the publication of this report was a massive consolidation of school districts across the country, eliminating most high schools with less than 200 students. This didn't affect Elkhorn High, which then had an enrollment of about 380 on the way to 400 and higher. But, in the fall of 1957, Delavan incorporated students of nearby Darien, and became Delavan-Darien High School. A year later, Genoa City joined Lake Geneva and became Badger High School. Schools also added "advanced placement" courses to the curriculum

The 1950s was a special time in the history of American education leaving fond memories for many students much of the time. The personal relationships and opportunities offered then at Elkhorn High seem old-fashioned now. Today, the school has over 1000 students, and like many others across the land it has become increasingly bureaucratic, socially stratified, and de-humanized. So much of schooling is routine in the service of order and control.

Discerning educators recognize that much has been lost in the growth of large schools and wish we could reclaim the high school of 300-500 students, along with comparable middle schools. But this would take more tax revenue than many Americans appear willing to provide. Much of schooling is about keeping kids out of the way and under surveillance, while testing them regularly to maintain the deception that this is an authentic indicator of learning.

For some students, particularly stars, "the king's and queens, duchesses and dukes," "life after high school" often finds stunted athletic lives. The highlight for various EHS athletes was on the football gridiron or hardwoods of the Kinne Gymnasium. Some attempted to continue athletic careers in college, but few succeeded. "Tiny" Millard ('46) failed to make the Wisconsin basketball squad, and coach Bud Foster may be responsible for coining the term "big, slow white guy." Those who did succeed typically attended small colleges and were top-notch students. Frank Eames, Bob Morrissey, and Bob Sorenson (class of 1947) played football at Division III colleges—Eames at Beloit, Morrissey at St. Norbert (near Green Bay), and Sorenson at Lawrence in Appleton. In a few years, Don Matheson ('49) and Wayne Welch ('51) would excel as football centers at Lawrence and La Crosse respectively.

Jerome Hart ('51) and Jerry Nettesheim ('54) also went on to college basketball—at Lawrence and St. Norbert respectively. Their more heralded teammates: Toby Clauer ('51), Gordy Babcock ('53) and Jim Platts ('55) would find "life after high school" a come down. Clauer had the talent to play Big Ten basketball at Wisconsin but left college after his freshman season for academic reasons. Likewise, Babcock and Platts had stunted college careers. In contrast, 6'3" Nettesheim, who taught and coached at EHS, was a superb college player.

Bob Piper, class of 1942, was an exception, who started in the 1943 Badger backfield, but World War II decimated those teams, and Piper left the varsity to concentrate on pre-med studies. Dick Grimm ('55), after two years in the Marines, played both ways on the Badger line from 1959-1961.

From nearby Delavan, Ron Smith ('54) played Big Ten basketball and baseball at Northwestern, while Whitewater's Steve Ambrose ('53) was a guard and linebacker at Wisconsin. Both Ambrose and Smith went on to university careers as history professors. Steven Ambrose was the well-known authority on military history and best-selling author of such books as *Citizen Soldiers, Band of Brothers, and Undaunted Courage.* He died from lung cancer in 2002.

Near the end of the 1950s and into the early 1960s, Jon Platts (Whitewater), Don Koepnick (River Falls), and Bill Lock (Stevens Point) played on Division III basketball teams in the Wisconsin state conference. Unlike today, a number of top-notch high school athletes from the Southern Lakes didn't go to college because then academic standards for athletes at big-time universities had a modicum of rigor. Today, a conspicuous double standard exists for athletes, and the "academy" is more accessible for them.

Another aspect of sports decades ago was the all-around participation of kids and versatility of athletes. Gone is the day of the triple-threat back and the four-sport player. Alan Van ('62) lettered four years each in baseball and track—as catcher behind the plate and running dashes while heaving the shot put and discus. On the gridiron, he played both ways as a fullback and linebacker, returned punts and kick offs, and was available to do the kicking. His senior year, he led the basketball team to a conference title. (He also may have erased chalk boards and laundered towels.)

The youngest Van was hardly alone: Elkhorn could point to Bob Piper ('42), Bill Morrissey ('46) Bob Hanny ('48), Bill Kehoe ('53) Jim Platts ('55), Jon Platts ('58) Don Koepnick ('59) and Jim Gray ('61) among others, who combined excellence with versatility. Kids nowadays specialize early, and many concentrate on one sport, often playing it year around, so that they might reach the "next level." This attitude mostly dwells on the future with its illusive pursuit of fame and money rather than enjoying the moment.

At the college and professional level, specialization and glorification has intensified. Big-time collegiate and professional football, for example, has lost a sense of play. The "game" has become an extension of the corporate industrial state with talk about programs and multiple staffing assignments. The head coach operates as Chief

Operating Officer on the field, while the A.D. (Athletic Director) is the CEO (Chief Executive Officer.) And the multi-faceted staff with coaches for every position act like division heads directing their minions on the field. As of this writing, the "weight training coach" for the University of Florida Gators is paid $300 thousand a year.

Football players go on and off the field like soldiers in battle, all with exclusive assignments: blocking backs, short-yardage runners, third-down receivers, wide outs, return specialists, as well as punters who do nothing else, and, "snappers." These guys hunch over the ball, like a big turtle, and "snap" it to a punter or holder. You may remember this as "hiking" the ball. Many of these people are part of "special teams," who add to disruptions, as if TV timeouts to sell products weren't enough. Place kickers, entering the game periodically, are like crafty salesmen who often determine the outcome and "seal the deal." Not infrequently these "soccer style" kickers become the most important player.

The game has drifted far from the 1960s and champion Green Bay Packers, where running back Paul Hornung also served as the placekicker. Ends Boyd Dowler and Max McGee handled the punting, defensive backs Herb Adderley and Willie Wood returned punts and kicks, and offensive guard Jerry Kramer kicked off. Much of the games "ebb and flow" has been lost to the dismay of traditionalists.

18 Distorted Priorities

Sports is that child we raised with money but not love,
who we allowed to grow up amid privilege but not
values except to win at all costs.
William C. Rhoden

C ompetitive sports have taken on a surrogate military role, and its language, particularly with football, is laced with war and military metaphors. Teams do battle, as the offense commences an air attack with the quarterback pulling the trigger to launch bombs, while linemen are in the trenches, and the defense blitzes linebackers and corner backs. Coaching staff, like corporate executives, set up war rooms and lay out strategies and tactics to contain the enemy. And everyone seems to "lock and load" these days to accomplish a mission.

Each year, we also witness an extravagant corporate ritual called the "Super Bowl." It's mass entertainment complete with over-the-top performances, sandwiched around a football contest that many pay little attention to, and punctuated by excessive, wasteful, and gaudy advertising. This display is especially inappropriate, as I write, at a time when excesses of the American financial, corporate and consumer culture have brought our nation's economic system and many workers to their knees.

Over the past several decades, television has increasingly gained more control over big-time NCAA sports, notably football and basketball at major universities. This is a far cry from the crisp autumn afternoons of my childhood when we would intermittently rake leaves and toss a football while listening on radio to the Badgers, led by All-American fullback Alan "The Horse" Ameche. Even then I sensed that intercollegiate sports colored the campus life of students, but assumed mostly for the good.

Over a half-century later, the distorting effects of big-time college sports have literally altered the nature of undergraduate education—mostly for ill. The impact of television is a sensible place to begin to understand this phenomenon. For those of us growing up in a sports culture, college football and basketball are great entertainment. TV networks figured this out long ago, cultivating immense corporate advertising and addicting the NCAA and universities to the revenue that flows from their sponsorship.

Michael Farber, writing in *Sports Illustrated*, explained how the corrupting impact of football at a university tears at its academic heart. Some schools have literally sold their souls to be major players throwing good money at a bad project. The effect is to siphon funds from libraries and laboratories, reduce staff, diminish the undergraduate curriculum, undermine the intellectual life of learning communities, and shortchange students.

University of Chicago President, Robert Hutchins, warned of this debasing effect in the early 1940s when the school's board of trustees pulled the Maroons out of the Big Ten Conference. Yet, few schools followed Hutchins' leadership. Even then football and basketball programs had a grip on the throats of many universities.

Division I college presidents tend to cite the financial support these sports bring from alumni, but for most schools (about 80 percent) the cost of financing highly competitive programs exceeds revenue.

Murray Sperber made the case in his book titled *Beer and Circus: How Big-time College Sports Is Crippling Undergraduate Education* (2004). Sperber, a professor of English and American Studies at Indiana University, drew the wrath of then IU basketball coach Bobby Knight and much of the school's student body for arguing, rather convincingly, that undergraduate education is much better off without big-time sports entertainment. The professor received little support from the IU president and administration who virtually were "in the pocket" of Knight. This is business as usual at many schools where the football or basketball coach is the most powerful person on campus, not to mention highest paid.

What Sperber documents in his book are how the ascent of big-time sports and the descent of undergraduate studies are intertwined. Many students, at most big universities these days, receive a feeble education, built on immense lecture classes, taught often by graduate assistants where little is expected of them. In turn, students are distracted from the intellectual life of a learning community by the games and partying, i.e., "beer and circus." As one reviewer remarked, "He (Sperber) is nothing less than the conscience for a vast entertainment industry that seems to have been born without one."

None of this intellectual and ethical ignominy had much impact on graduating from EHS in the late fifties. At Beloit College, I played on the football and track teams, but was a student first and athlete next, which is an apt description of "student-athlete." At schools like Beloit, athletic teams depart for an out-of-town contest after all the players have completed their classes for the day. I graduated in 1961 holding the school's pass catching record and as a member of four relay teams, whose records still stand after 50 years.

Yet, my achievements on the track came with the tremendous support of teammates. At Elkhorn High, it was Roger Van who anchored the relay teams and was most responsible for their record setting performances. Later, at Beloit, I was fortunate to run four years in the company of Harv Flodin, a 220 and 440-yard sprinter, who left the college with several enduring track records. Flodin, an attorney in Southern California, and I, now in Colorado, remain good friends sharing engaging ideas related to economics, politics, foreign policy, and the challenges of life in general.

Relay events, of course, are not won by one or two people, and I'm indebted to several teammates who made possible a memorable career in track and field. At EHS these runners were Bill Ward, Bill Riese, and Ron Pearsall as well as my younger brother. At Beloit, given the number of record-setting teams, the list is longer and includes Rick Chase, Jon Parvin, Don Fisher, Jim Hedrich, and Daryl Hessel in addition to Flodin. Parvin, from Fort Edwards just outside Wisconsin Rapids, captained the football team our senior year. In the summer of 1956, we ran one-two in the 100-yard dash at Badger Boys State. While I raced in canvas warm-ups, Jon scampered down the track in Winnebago moccasins.

Roger Van was sought after by a number of colleges to compete in track and field, and chose Marquette University mainly for its academic program. Marquette was the lone dental school in Wisconsin, and he desired a career in this field. Attending Marquette rather than the University of Wisconsin, for example, made the transition from undergraduate studies to dental school seamless for someone with good grades.

He was the only full-scholarship athlete at Marquette outside the basketball program. As history relates, Marquette, as with many Catholic universities, terminated its football program at the end of Van's junior year and with it track and field. The expense of maintaining highly competitive sports programs, as the stakes grew, was not fiscally prudent for the private, Jesuit school. Like DePaul, St. Johns, Fordham, Georgetown, Providence, and similar universities, Marquette concentrated its intercollegiate athletics on basketball, which is more cost-effective.

Yet, Roger made the most of a two-year varsity career at Marquette running 9.6 seconds in 100 and 20.7 in 220 his last and junior year. Only a nagging hamstring kept him from winning the 220 and a triple sprint victory in the premier Central Collegiate Conference Meet in 1961 (after capturing the 100-yard dash and anchoring the winning 4x100 relay) and competing in the NCAA finals.

There indeed has been life after high school and beyond. As the graduation slogan for the EHS Class of 1957 reads, "Our Best is Yet to Come." Yet, high school days included sweet memories that we draw on as life in the global, high-tech, fast-communications world becomes increasingly abstract, institutional, and distant. It is a rootedness in the values and relative simplicity of the past that remind us who we are and what is important.

As testimony to the enduring lessons of sport learned in an "age of innocence" and a liberal arts environment, I've maintained an active, sporting life. A need for physical activity and introspection were parlayed into distance running as an adult. The sprinter in me found a reservoir of "slow-twitch" muscle fibers and the ability to run a wide range of distances.

In graduate school at the University of Colorado in the late 1960s, I ran with the university track team;

later on the faculty at Grinnell College, I trained with the cross-country and track teams. During tenure in South Florida, I became an accomplished road racer as a master competitor. This range is reflected in a collection of personal bests over two decades from a 100-yard dash time of 9.9 seconds in college to 32:44 minutes for 10 kilometers at age 41—with a string of comparable times at distances in between and beyond. Running is a form of therapy.

♪

Liberal arts education has been dismantled for decades, and many of our universities have become high-priced occupational training centers. This even was reflected in the sentiment of parents and many friends a half century ago when I went to the college. The question often was "What are you going to do with your education? They viewed learning in utilitarian terms as a vocational pursuit. Prestigious universities and business schools, Hedges writes, are producing "uncreative bureaucrats superbly trained to carry out systems management," who see only piecemeal solutions to satisfy corporate goals focused on numbers and profits. They lack a moral and intellectual core. As a result, our nation is becoming less equipped to meet the challenges of modern economic society.

19 **Lost Innocence**

*Our lives begin to end the day we become silent about
things that matter.*
Martin Luther King Jr.

A mark of an educated person is the ability to stand
on the edge of culture and see it from an outsider's
perspective. Nineteenth century German philosopher
Johann Wolfgang von Goethe expressed this nicely in
a poem: "If you want me to show you the vicinity, you
must first climb to the roof."

The United States, writes conservative columnist
David Brooks, has been conspicuous for one trait: manic
energy. "Americans work longer hours than any other
people. We switch jobs more frequently, move more
often, earn more and consume more." Most accept this
as the "conventional wisdom"—just the way it is.

A half-century earlier, historian Richard Hofstadter
said much the same, more critically, in his Pulitzer-
Prize book, *Anti-intellectualism in American Life* (1964).
He accused religion, politics, and the public schools
of fostering in people resentment and suspicion of
intellect and a life of the mind. Small-town preachers,
businessmen, and lawyers, in particular, mask their
bias against intellect with the rhetoric of morality, utility,

and practicality. Our "Commercial Republic," as Brooks labels it, excels at creating wealth and products, but is built on a fundamentalist substructure that devalues the rational and has a contempt for evidence. This ethos gets us in trouble!

President George W. Bush, for example, sold a gullible public on the existence of Iraqi WMDs (Weapons of Mass Destruction) and took the country to war on false premises. Sufficient evidence, particularly in non-mainstream media, existed to cast serious doubt on the Administrations assertions, but a co-opted press and intellectually lazy public went along with the deception.

Technology has always been an integral part of American life from the printing press and telegraph to the telephone, radio, railway, automobile, television, computer, cell phone, Internet and more. Americans define "progress" as advances in technology, and with instantaneous communications, the pace has sped up considerably for today's youth. They live in a so-called "24-7" infotainment culture that has an immense potential for learning but much of it is "mindless" entertainment. Our culture has "a romance with technology," explains social critic Susan Jacoby, and we don't understand that computers are just tools that don't make us smarter.

As media analyst, Neil Postman, explains, "Technopoly is the only form of technology that Americans have known. It creates a society only loosely controlled by social custom and religious tradition and is driven by the impulse to invent." Schools, we are told, teach "technology education" but it is really "technology training." What we all need to know is not just *how to use technology* but *how technology uses us*. This is what Postman meant by "technopoly" and the control it can hold on culture and over our lives.

I doubt if a "golden age of education" ever existed, as some label the 1950s and 1960s, but research suggests that students then had greater attention spans, a modest sense of entitlement, and less need for immediate gratification. Modern life has taken us down a road of "cultural ignorance"—an immense and embarrassing ignorance of science, history, the Constitution, and economics.

High schools have caved into the mass culture, and teachers find ways to circumvent the rigors of sustained and demanding scholarship. Gone are the days of Mark Thachery (*To Sir with Love, 1967*), Jean Brodie (*The Prime of Miss Jean Brodie, 1969*), and John Keaton (*Dead Poets Society, 1989*) or even Elkhorn High's Sam Kaplan and Ruth Bushman. Nevertheless, it is my experience, having founded a charter high school in Colorado and worked with students that one does not have to dig deeply to find desire for intellectual engagement. Students today are mentally starved in their superficial culture just as a thirsty person is in the desert.

Remaining innocent, of course, is undesirable, and one must eventually become an adult, but just growing older doesn't make this so. One function of a good society is that the young move into adulthood with qualities of a mature person. This means that they acquire character as defined by the pursuit of knowledge and delayed gratification; a strong work ethic and service; humility, conscience, reflection, and the pursuit of truth as a primary guide.

Modern society, however, fails in much of this, and the young are provided only the shell of a rich culture defined by its consumer economy. By the 21st century, we managed to create a dubious environment for growing up: As a result mostly of "technopoly," childhood prematurely disappears, while adolescence extends often into a person's thirties.

♪

Perhaps, above all else, maturity means "to know thyself," which in ancient Hebrew tradition is the essence of "conversion"—not dependency, guilt, sin, and redemption, as understood in traditional Christian culture.

A place to begin this quest, for those of any age, is to regain more contact with nature. Walking, hiking, bicycling, jogging, gardening, and any number of sporting activities allow the human spirit to "commune with nature," which includes self, and to "live life large." Wilderness puts us in touch with our core identity and nurtures the soul. Our great national parks create happiness. They are democratic experiments in nature, remarked President Roosevelt.

Many of us are confined in offices and other structures too much of the time. This is not a natural habitat of humans; for tens of thousands of years, we were inexorably connected with nature. Along with various conveniences, modern living presents hazards to our mental and spiritual well-being. Many people are like caged animals confined in a zoo slowly going mad. So, we seek solace through shopping or consumerism, which is counterproductive for the human spirit, or worse turn to destructive, anti-social behavior.

For the young, in particular, schooling could be reconstructed, so that all are educated in small, personal environments. One aspect would be creating high schools in which *every student participates in genuine physical activity*—an intra- or interscholastic sport each season—fall, winter, and spring. Life at Elkhorn High through the 1950s had some of this quality but fell short. Schools were convivial, but sports' programs minimal. For boys in these "Happy Days", it was football in the fall (no soccer and cross country), only basketball in the winter (no wrestling or volleyball), with baseball and tennis in spring until track was added. Like the old-fashion ice cream parlor, no 31 flavors were available, just "vanilla, chocolate, and strawberry."

Girls—females and women—were not yet allowed to exhibit their "natural superiority" to borrow from humanist, Ashley Montagu (incidentally a male, British anthropologist.) Today, boys and girls alike participate in many school sports activities. But most schools now are both so large and competitive that only the elite compete at the varsity level. Children face a vicious "pyramid of participation" as they advance through the years from universal involvement in the early grades to only the select few by senior high. Or schools take a "laissez-faire" approach that allows kids to retreat to the tyranny of shopping malls, oppression of dead-end jobs, and seclusion of electronic gadgets.

Creating smaller, convivial schools is hardly a fanciful idea, if communities had the will. To finish the cliché, there is a way: reallocate economic resources to create these environments. A view around the Southern Lakes, for example, and its schools suggests considerable wealth. Elkhorn, Badger, Big Foot, Burlington, and many other schools reflect the region's abundance with its rich landscape, fertile farmland, and ample property values. Walworth County experienced increases in farm land values as did other regions of the country during the past 40 years. As farming became more profitable and urban development pushed out into hinterlands, creating "exurbs," land values soared. Early on, this drove out the marginal farmer who could not afford taxes on his land. Those with the resources and skills reaped "windfall" gains when they consolidated into larger farms, leased the land, or sold to developers.

Wealth exists to support such schools, if we could escape the mindset driven by "efficiency measures" and "economies of scale" that are a primary rationale for large schools.

Gone are small public high schools that existed in the 1950s—Sharon, Darien, Walworth, Genoa City—all consolidated into larger districts. Only Williams Bay High stands as a monument to antiquity. The history of school consolidations dates to the "Cold War" and the nation's desire to have larger schools, rigorous curriculum, a stronger economy, and more powerful military—all to counter the Soviet Union. This was accomplished to the detriment of many students who increasingly had to negotiate intense and bureaucratic big-school environments with the loss of intimacy and involvement. But it does serve to field more competitive sports for the few.

Most of the current Southern Lakes Conference high schools compete in Division I interscholastic sports programs with enrollments of 1000 and more students, a threshold that EAHS (now Elkhorn Area High School) surpassed in 2008. The environment has changed considerably over the decades. Nevertheless, one wonders if graduates are any better prepared for college, communities, and the workforce—as scholars, citizens, and artisans respectively.

Yes, records have fallen, but no one has managed to eclipse the long jump and 220-yard school marks set by Roger Van over a half century ago. And who would bet against any of the three Elk sprint relay foursomes from the mid-1950s, running against modern teams on a comparable track?

20 Warrior Society

Blessed are the peacemakers, for they shall be called the children of God.
Jesus' Sermon on the Mount

All five of the Van Scotter brothers served in the military, and my experience started in Newport, Rhode Island. I then was stationed in the San Francisco Bay area, but all of my three-year tour of duty was on board ship in the Western Pacific—Japan, the Philippines, and Vietnam. Navy days proved to be an extension of my liberal arts education. A person's education, properly pursued, only begins in school and college. It is the rest of learning in life that counts, if one is to become enlightened in any sense of the word.

Schooling itself often becomes indoctrination and is seen largely in vocational terms. Here, studies are mostly instrumental aimed at providing a degree with which a person can get work and earn money. Genuine education, however, is the opposite in which it enhances a person's capacity to live more simply and enjoy cultural, environmental, and intellectual pleasures. These pursuits generally are inexpensive, demanding principally reflection, thoughtfulness, patience, and aesthetic sensibilities.

A good education also prepares one to be a loving critic of society. During my first year on the West Coast, I boarded a military flight heading east. My destination was New Orleans and the wedding of Frank and Susan McClellan, where I was to be the "best man." The aircraft took me as far as Birmingham, Alabama; from there I would travel by bus to the Crescent city. Arriving in my khaki officer's uniform, I entered a dingy ticket station only to realize that I was on the "colored people's" side. The white ticket agent, probably, detecting that I was a clueless northern boy, motioned me to the "white's only" terminal, which was much more presentable. I declined indicating that I would purchase a ticket right here.

I departed this segregated environment immediately and took a short walk before returning to the bus. When I boarded, it was virtually full, and I took a seat in the back with the "negroes." A white passenger motioned me to the front of the bus, but I again declined. What saved me, I suspect, was respect for the uniform. Yet, the racist environment that I encountered in the South was not so distant from behavior that I witnessed at Elkhorn High. During the mid-1950s when civil rights became a social issue, I was labeled by some students in class as a "nigger lover" for defending equality for blacks. I was in good company, for this was the insult given President John F. Kennedy, particularly by those who celebrated his assassination.

Through military service, notably the tour in Vietnam, and "lifelong learning," I became skeptical of war, expansionism, and U.S. foreign policy. Military duty prompted me to ask questions of war, and liberal (as in liberating) thought helped to decipher the fog that tends to accompany the "heat of battle." I've learned that Americans are ambivalent towards war, both glorifying and horrified by it.

We also prize the idea of the *citizen soldier* but are reluctant to draft citizens into the military. As a result, the United States tends to have a mercenary or volunteer army that can compromise cherished democratic principles. Yet, an army can hardly be considered voluntary when most enlistees come from society's underclass in which military service often represents their best and sometimes only employment opportunity.

Our nation also claims to fight only wars of defense while engaging in wars of aggression. In doing so, we profess to believe in just wars but often build a mythology around war to justify its action. The Mexico War in the mid-1800s was an imperialist conflict to expand the nation's borders and extend power. Later, in that century, the United States fought the Spanish American War to open markets and advance economic growth.

Over time, our government also supported foreign dictators and regimes with policies antithetical to this nation's principles, but who could serve corporate economic interests. U.S. forces overthrew democratically elected governments in Iran (1953) and Guatemala (1954), along with Chile (1973). Beginning in 1979, the CIA attempted to undermine a legitimate Sandinista government in Nicaragua. This took an ill-fated turn in 1985 with the Iran-Contra debacle.

Vietnam was not a war to defend liberty against a nefarious foreign aggressor. Nor was Korea before it and Iraq recently. We don't have to scratch the surface deeply to see that these military ventures were much about securing regional power and markets. U.S. foreign policy during the Cold War, as outlined by diplomat George Kennan, centered on *containment*. The policy explains U.S. action in Southeast Asia for the purpose of containing Soviet expansion. Kennan, however, took issue with hard line and "hawkish" policymakers in Washington who supported military build-up. He had spent many years in the Moscow embassy and understood that Russian rulers were "neurotic, insecure, and fearful of comparisons with the West."

For Kennan, a Princeton graduate and Milwaukee native, the objective of U.S. foreign policy should be access to resources and markets around the world, if we are to maintain a high standard of living. This has led to considerable mischief as the United States came to support regimes in Latin America and elsewhere that allows U.S. corporations a privileged position, even if it meant supporting strong, autocratic leaders. To realists, such as Kennan, the United States should not respond with vague, idealistic slogans about human rights, raising living standards, and democratization. George Kennan, however, bears some responsibility for the specious "domino theory" that prompted the U.S. Government to engage in a devastating war in Vietnam, a small, subsistence farming nation. If one country falls to the communists, others will follow!

This is not to diminish the humanitarian aid, this country has provided for many across the globe in the former Yugoslavia, Somalia, and elsewhere. And it certainly is not to dismiss noble battles, such as those against Fascism in World War II that our nation fought to resist "evil" and secure "freedom." Yet, both terms are cheapened when carelessly used to justify all U.S. military intervention—the imperialistic and righteous alike.

War, writes author and correspondent Chris Hedges, "is a force that gives us meaning." "The rush of battle," he continues, "is a potent and often lethal addiction, for war is a drug .... It is peddled by mythmakers— historians, war correspondents, film makers, novelists, and the state—all of whom endow it with qualities it does not possess: excitement, eroticism, power, chances to rise above our small stations in life, and a bizarre fantastic universe that has grotesque and dark beauty.... The enduring attraction of war is this: Even with its destruction and carnage, it can give us what we long for in life. It can give purpose, meaning, and a reason for living. Only when we are in the midst of conflict does the shallowness and vapidness of much of our lives become apparent. Trivia dominates our conversations and increasingly our airwaves. And war is an enticing elixir. It gives us resolve, a cause. It allows us to be noble."

These are powerful words shared at some length, because this message of a warrior society permeated the culture of Middle America in the 1950s. Not a national holiday passed without a patriotic and nationalist parade through the streets of Elkhorn, Wisconsin complete with marching bands, veterans of foreign wars, and a prancing horse leading the way. It was a conventional and narrow version of patriotism. Ironically, military service, war, and reflection helped to transform my political philosophy and direction in life.

Not all veterans come away from the military in a sound state of mind. Many of us know the soldier returning from war who remains silent almost catatonic at what he witnessed and maybe did. Bob Morrissey, quarterback of the championship 1946 team and accomplished defensive back in college, became a career Army officer after graduating from St. Norbert. He served in both Korea and Vietnam. As with many other soldiers, war took an emotional toll. The EHS athlete turned to alcohol for relief and was left with a shattered life.

Bellicose often is rooted in fear. The *Utne Reader* included a story not long ago about an American hailing a cab in Boston, as I recall. Noting the driver's strong Russian accent, he asked, "So what do you think of America?"

Hesitant at first, the driver finally blurted out, "You Americans are all afraid." Afraid, what is he talking about? We Americans are the most powerful nation in the world. Just then a BMW and Mercedes sped past the cab. "Those people are the most afraid," he said, gesturing at the cars. "Afraid they will lose it." "In Russia, we fear the KGB," he added. "Here, you don't trust anyone. You are afraid of each other."

We lock up everything for fear that it will be stolen. Growing up as a child our homes were seldom if ever locked. Shops didn't do a brisk business in bicycle locks, because we didn't feel the need for such security. Of course, we built bomb shelters and held practice alerts in case the Russians were to attack, but eventually got over this paranoia.

Boarding an airplane nowadays, we run a gauntlet of security measures where a nail file and lotion bottle are treated as lethal weapons. An alarming number of citizens arm themselves with hand guns and protect their homes with sophisticated security systems. Now, I understand that every home should have an "emergency world band radio in the event of hurricanes, tornadoes, earthquakes, electric power outages, and terrorist attacks." Supposedly, this is a "homeland security" recommendation, but I suspect it is little more than an advertiser looking for another sucker.

Advertising also plays on our fear of not being thin enough, young enough, and beautiful—or being too bald, wrinkled, impotent, or just ordinary. The war in Iraq added to this fear-based environment. Fear is a form of control—not so much the kind that George Orwell spoke of as "Big Brother" in *1984*, but the more insidious variety that Aldous Huxley wrote about in *Brave New World*, which is more difficult to detect.

In his book *Amusing Ourselves to Death* (1985), Neil Postman described the contrast this way: "What Orwell feared were those who would ban books. What Huxley feared was that there would be no reason to ban a book, for there would be no one who wanted to read one. Orwell feared those who would deprive us of information. Huxley feared those who would give us so much that we would be reduced to passivity and egoism. Orwell feared that the truth would be concealed from us. Huxley feared the truth would be drowned in a sea of irrelevance. Orwell feared we would become a captive culture. Huxley feared we would become a trivial culture...."

Many people purchase SUVs or some large vehicle for safety. Of course, this can be counterproductive where everyone feels compelled to escalate and buy bigger. It seems the more we have, the more we fear. The more affluent are choosing to live within "gated communities," which mostly serves to separate them from the greater community.

Many Americans may be living well, but if the firm goes under or one is laid off, the economic safety net is weak or non-existent. Without sufficient investment in our nation's common wealth, e.g., income maintenance and health care, we are vulnerable to vagaries of the economy, fearful, and without imagination. As Robert F. Kennedy, then Attorney General warned, "the grip of timidity prevents us from embracing the future and approaching it creatively."

This desire for more and bigger also aggravates economic problems. The United States witnessed periodic economic crashes over the past few decades: the housing bubble of the 1980s was followed by the Savings & Loan Crisis and the 1991 recession. After the technology bubble of 1990s came the 2001 recession. Less than a decade later, our economy felt the "Crash of 2008." The U.S. model of growth has been based on overconsumption and lack of savings. Americans borrowed too much. Too much human capital went into finance than more productive activities, such as investing in the public and private infrastructure. Most of the nation's over spending was for unproductive assets—the greatest of these being housing. Too many spurious subprime mortgages and too many houses

4,000 square feet and larger. We have cultivated a false sense of "living large."

The response often received when asked—why? Why larger homes and yards than one needs, or more cars, clothes, equipment and technology than used? The answer often heard is the moral equivalent of what William Jefferson Clinton said about his Monica Lewinsky tryst—"Because I could!" Maybe so, but the nation, economy, and environment can't.

It's not surprising that many people hear the call to retreat into private lives, go along, keep quiet, and be invisible. But this presents a big problem. Living in fear robs us of life and diminishes living. Fear forces us to "live small rather than large." And education, properly understood, prepares us to trust our unique talent, tap into personal gifts, and live large. Our species has made it where we are today by being adventurous, taking risks, solving problems, and boldly creating.

Love and fear cannot coexist or occupy the same space. We tend to think that opposite of love is hate, but not so. The opposite of love is fear.

♪

This military temper is dissipating: the wealthier a nation and the more evenly incomes distributed, the less likely people are to support pre-emptive wars and universal conscription. Nations need an underclass to fight wars. When George W. Bush started the Iraqi War, he asked little except of the soldiers, who did the fighting, and their families. Others were told to "go shopping," and few Americans were actually touched by war. Had he been honest with the American public and announced that everyone would contribute—taxes raised to pay the cost and a draft reinstated—that would have been the end of this military venture. The absence now of patriotic parades in Elkhorn is telling.

In 1789, the U.S. government established a War Department, also known as the War Office. In 1947 it was renamed the Department of the Army then became the Department of Defense in 1949. "News satirist," Steven Colbert might label this "truthiness." For affluent Americans, war is obsolete, or at least being played with different ground rules. Sports have become the modern citizens' surrogate for aggression, hostility, and militarism. We still are warriors only with a different venue.

The United States is building a military presence in Afghanistan with a private mercenary force. We are "privatizing" war with contractors from firms such as Blackwater Security Consulting, who are carrying out government operations. Our government also is "sanitizing" war using drones from afar with so-called surgical attacks that nonetheless take the lives of innocent civilians. The ethical implications of this are immense, and such operations undermine democracy and violate international treaties.

The United States is the largest seller of arms and munitions on the planet. We have over 750 military bases to maintain around the globe, and U.S. military spends more than all other militaries on earth combined. More than half of the discretionary federal budget goes to the military. Our nation has developed an entrenched *war economy* that is a huge drain on national resources. When a weapon is fired, tank destroyed, or plane downed, the product is gone—not to mention the life of a cherished and productive human being.

Some cite the economic stimulus of war spending that creates thousands of jobs and can be the "life blood" of a community. This spending, however, doesn't create productive assets in the way that a new manufacturing plant, school, hospital, bridge, and high-speed rail system does. Military spending provides a short-term jolt to the body politic much as alcohol or nicotine does to the human body. With this, local economies become dependent on the "drug of war."

Two aspects of war during my youth also had considerable impact. In February 1942, 110,000 Japanese-Americans were arrested without warrants and legal proceedings and moved into ten internment camps in seven states. This, our country did out of racism and unexamined fear. Many children of these citizens were sent to stay in Wisconsin, and Jo Icke, a high school girl, lived with the Van Scotter family. For my parents, this took courage and helped them to overcome areas of xenophobia.

During the early 1950s, towns and cities across the country built bomb shelters in response to the so-called "Red Scare." This too was manufactured fear that also led to revising the Pledge of Allegiance during this anti-Communist, "godless" frenzy with its impact on civil liberties. The original pledge written in 1892 included the words, "...One Nation indivisible, with liberty and justice for all."

In June 1954, the words "under God" were inserted after "One Nation." Nearly 50 years later, in response to a challenge made in California, the Ninth Circuit Court of Appeals (2002) ruled that adding "under God" amounted to an unconstitutional endorsement of religion. Indignation prevailed across the land! President Bush called the ruling ridiculous, and Congress voted unanimously to pass a resolution in support of the pledge. Although many constitutional scholars haled the decision, no one in Congress had the courage to point out the contradiction in the words, "One Nation, under God, indivisible."

How possibly can a nation of Jews, Buddhists, agnostics, atheists, humanists, and other non-believers as well as Christians be both "indivisible and under God"? This modification of history would not have been viewed kindly by the first six presidents of

United States—those gentlemen responsible for writing the *Declaration of Independence* and conceiving the Constitution. They were Deistic rationalists who had nothing against spiritually, but their God was one with nature. Jefferson and others believed that the clergy and organized religion, neglected reason in favor of the supernatural.

Perhaps, this nation's finest accomplishment over time has been to assimilate waves of immigrants representing many nationalities, races, ethnic groups, religions, and cultures. To achieve such unity, while enriching our culture with diversity, is something no other country can claim. Why would a noble nation occasionally employ divisive measures that undermine the Constitution and civil liberties of some citizens because they are a minority?

As I write, the *2009 American Religious Identification Survey* reports the number of Americans who claim no religious affiliation has doubled since 1990, rising from eight to 15 percent. The percentage of self-identified Christians also has fallen 10 points since 1990, from 86 to 76 percent. The so-called Judeo-Christian consensus is giving away to a post-modern, post-Christian, and post-Western culture.

In 1922, Elkhorn, Wisconsin awarded the nation's first American Legion Medal to a high school graduate. Among other things, this is testimony to the patriotic and military spirit of this conservative town. Alan, Roger, and Richard were recipients of this honor. Each summer the local American Legion Post also sponsors two incoming senior boys to attend a week at Badger Boys State on the campus of Ripon College. Again, three of us—Don, Roger and Richard—were selected. The other participant in the summer of 1956 was Paul Paddock, Mike's cousin. In this venture too, young women were "shortchanged," but one from the class of '57—Pat Tripp—did attend Badger Girls State.

The examined life is a greater elixir than war and sports. This we know from the teachings of Socrates and Jesus, among others, but ignore at immense personal peril.

21 Team Play

A relay race is a team sport but then so is living in a community. We are in this together, and cooperation is crucial. Take something as common as driving your automobile in town or on the highway. When it goes smoothly, drivers behave as teammates. But in our highly individualistic society, this readily breaks down as drivers look for an edge, are distracted, curse others, and flash obscene hand gestures.

We Americans embrace working in teams, on battlefields, and in community projects, yet glorify the reclusive hero. This was drilled home in '50s movies through characters such as the Lone Ranger, Shane, and James Dean. The rugged individual in forms as different as the trailblazing explorer, lone homesteader, business magnate, swashbuckling athlete, and reclusive poet has captured the American Spirit. Tension between a need for fellowship and the lonely road weighs heavily.

Rampant individualism today comes in many forms, including the kid who thinks that school exists just to give him skills and knowledge to get a high-paying job and the adult who wants his taxes lower saying "I earned it and it's my money, so keep your hands off." Neither sees himself as "citizens" of an institution they are both part of and indebted to—be a school, city, or nation. This attitude has not been good for our republic.

As social beings, we seek the company of and collaboration with others. Yet, community has perennially been at odds with the spirit of individualism etched deeply in the national character. We often succumb to the false dichotomy that competition and cooperation are incompatible. Both hold the potential to enhance personal well-being, when properly understood. Competition can serve to bring out the best in foe and self alike, while cooperation accomplishes what cannot be done alone.

A distinctive high school moment came at the end of my junior year when English teacher Carol Bartingale thanked me for contributions to her class. I was flattered but more importantly realized that she was conveying a vital message: Our school and class couldn't work unless students, as well as teachers, took ownership in it. Ms. Bartingale, in effect, said that I had been a "student" and a citizen of her class.

I capped a running career in my late 50s and early 60s by helping to organize a 12-person team to run Oregon's "Hood-to-Coast Relay," a 196-mile race. This we did for six consecutive years. The race starts on Mt. Hood and ends at the Pacific Coast in Seaside. Old running mates from South Florida, New England, Colorado, and Oregon came together for this grueling relay that took our team 22 to 23 hours to complete. In some respects, this was an ultimate team experience and joy in running. In 2002, we fielded two teams, one of them a mixture of six women and six men – all over the age of 50. This was joyful because we all acted as "citizens," who were in the race together.

My team play began in 1947 and what can be described as "Friendly Indian" days. I was in 3rd grade and not yet old enough to join the team, but Don was a high school senior and assistant coach. In the final game of the season-ending tournament at Walworth High School, the young Elks had a comfortable lead with less than a minute remaining. Don signaled for me to take off my street shoes and check into play. I only had one pair, and they were not exactly $125 Nike "Air Jordans." So I entered the game in stocking feet with 30 seconds remaining on the clock and our team controlling the ball. With time running down, Rod Thorson, a 6th grader, set me up with a charitable pass, and I launched a 16-footer, that rippled the net with a resounding "swish."

This was a magic moment in the life of an 8-year-old. On a recent summer visit and stop in Walworth, I spotted the old high school across the town square. I crossed the park and peered into the school window. I promptly was intercepted by a suspicious assistant principal. Upon hearing my story, I could feel her heart melt. She opened the door and led me to the gym. It is beautiful and exactly as it was 60 years ago. Big Foot High today is less than a mile away, but the old school still stands. Tradition matters.

Thinclads is about a high school 880-yard relay team, but it drifts in and out of sports, society, and culture because this is life. Also indispensible to making sense of life is humor. "A sense of humor," philosopher William James reminds us, "is just common sense dancing." I trust my story provides some humor and common sense.

It is disquieting to realize that the American Legion Medal winners who preceded me at EHS in the mid-1950s have each passed away: Rod Thorson ('54), Jim Platts ('55), and Bill Ward ('56). We understand that genetics is significant in determining longevity. Fred MaGill was going strong when he lost his life to a work-related accident in 1945—at about the age I am now. Perhaps, Dad, who witnessed nearly three centuries of living (from July 1901 to December 1999), will leave my brothers and me one more gift.

Personally, I don't want such longevity with the assistance of heroic technology. We are told, and think accurately, that in the United States 20 percent of the population uses 80 percent of the medical dollars. More significantly, at least 30 percent of all Medicare costs are incurred during the last year of a person's life. Given this trend, our medical system is unsustainable. The answer to this contradiction will not come from the medical profession, whose responsibility is to keep people alive. The courage to die gracefully and naturally must come from within each and everyone one of us and with the help of spiritual and philosophical guidance, if so desired. This is a moral act and the ultimate team play.

We all have a script or narrative to help order and guide our lives. Joseph Campbell, master storyteller and soul guide, referred to them as *myths*, while Sigmund Freud, who understood our psychic needs better than anyone else, labeled such tales *illusions*.

Growing up in the 1950s was mythological and a time when illusions were held with ease. In the media, family life was portrayed idyllically through *Father Knows Best*, *Ozzie and Harriet*, and other TV shows. It was easy to think that "mine" was the only dysfunctional family, while all around people struggled "behind closed doors." Today, life's challenges are more transparent. I could have chosen many stories, aside from the family doctor with "wonderful bedside manners" and the handsome baseball player to help illustrate the ideology of small-town America. But, this essentially is a story about a relay team and young athletes within a community that touched my life.

I use the term "dysfunctional" in a general sense, with no disrespect meant, but raising a family of five energetic boys was no small task and one beyond the capability of many parents. Without the daily assistance of a maternal grandmother, Maud MaGill, I cringe to think what the state of our household might have been. Grandma lived a few blocks away and daily made the pilgrimage to assist mother in cleaning and other indispensable chores. Dad was a great guy, appreciated by all, but without the support of two older brothers, who served as surrogate fathers, life for Roger, Alan, and me would have suffered. This gives us all the more respect for Bob and Don who negotiated the Great Depression and World War II years under far more austere conditions than we experienced in the 1950s.

Call them what you will, but the point is that we need to create histories and futures for ourselves through narratives and stories. *Thinclads* is a story that gives meaning to my life. This meaning recognizes that all of us bring unique talents or gifts to our world. But they are just that—"gifts" that we've been given be it intelligence, artistic ability, engaging personality, physical attractiveness, intrapersonal awareness, longevity, or magnificent psychomotor skills, such as being the fastest runner in the state of Wisconsin. We don't own them and can't take credit for this talent; they were given to us. What we do own is the use we make of talents—that's called character. And character is another theme of my story.

In looking back, I'm struck by the contrast in vocations and life styles of my EHS teammates. Bill Ward was a college teacher; Roger Van a dentist and pilot; Bob Klitzkie, an attorney and senator, while Bill Riese worked road construction and Jim Wuttke was a lineman and cable splicer for the phone company. Just as on the ball field, the latter do the "heavy lifting" in life and are the backbone of economic society.

Without crisp blocking from Wuttke, Dave Fink, and Don Riese, Roger Van could not have performed his gridiron heroics. Without the work these guys also do for our economy, Mike Paddock couldn't prosper as a "gentleman farmer," Frank Eames couldn't put out a newspaper, Jon Platts couldn't serve as school superintendent, and I sure as hell couldn't enjoy the life of an academic and writer. We were "dependent upon one another then," and, though miles apart, we've been "in it together" over the years.

Communities are the basic building blocks of the republic, and they shift over time. New communities are being formed constantly as people travel to meetings and "surf" the Internet. The average American today moves every five years. Culture is being refashioned by the Internet just as television and radio had done earlier. People in the modern version of community increasingly live fractured lives in places geographically dispersed.

In writing this story, I talked with teammates, and friends, some of whom I had not communicated with for 50 years. All seemed eager to share memories, particularly of coaches. Every SLC school had at least one: For Delavan it was Wally Zimmerman, Don Breidenbach, and the venerable Webb Schultz, who pitched ever so briefly for the Chicago White Sox in 1924. Whitewater had Jim Crummy and Ken Nehring; Lake Geneva, Walter Jonas and Duane Morris; East Troy, John Schumann; Mukwonago, Cal Danielson; Wilmot, Frank Bucci; Harvard, Dan Horn; and Burlington, Harry "Dinty" Moore, Joan's father. Several of these men have a football field or basketball court named in their honor, including Elkhorn's remarkable Fred Suchy.

One myth embedded in our conventional wisdom is the Horatio Alger story of success. This tells that the talented individual through a meritocratic system can be a great success. What I've learned is that not all talented people become great successes, and most successful people have received a great deal of help along the way from family, culture, government, history, geography, good fortunes of birth, and friendships. Yet, sports represent culture's most meritocratic environment. One cannot fake a 400-meter dash or mile run. The best inevitably "rise to the top." As Voltaire said, "Illusion is the first of all pleasures."

Those "dealt a real bad hand" in life—children of abuse, alcohol, and poverty—need someone to "toss them a lifeline," writes author Joe Queenan in his compelling memoir *Closing Time*. No one is saved without that exceptional teacher, neighbor, employer, priest, or coach. Yet, one still must "swim to that lifeline" and do the hard work in life.

As I've explained to my own children—Shannon, Philip, and Caitlin—when their life goals seemed daunting, "Stay the course; if it were easy, everyone could do it."

22 Running

Most things in life have purpose, but not meaning.
Play is the direct opposite. It has no purpose but gives
meaning to life.
George Sheehan, runner, writer, and cardiologist

Memories of my boyhood often involved running: chasing a brother around the yard, running bases in a ballgame, pursuing a fly ball, playing football in the street or neighbor's field, dashing about in a game of tag, and hurdling over hedges along the backyards of homes lining the north 100-block of Washington and Lincoln streets.

I also remember returning home from the movies on a Friday night in the dark. At first the lights of downtown showed the way, but as I approached Washington, darkness took over and imaginary villains sprang from behind the huge maple and elm trees. I would break into a sprint, reaching our house just in time to leap safely onto the lighted front porch. It was an exhilarating dash that in retrospect would be preparation for races and long jump contests in high school and college.

Images of an amusing event at age nine will remain forever. It was a beautiful spring morning when I entered the kitchen as Dad was preparing his plumbing truck for the day's work, and mother had yet to come downstairs. Dad inevitably had several bottles of Pabst Blue Ribbon beer in the refrigerator waiting for his return after work. I should have known that he kept an exact count of the number of PBRs cooling, but this morning I took my chances and sipped six ounces, after which I slipped the half-full bottle into the back of the refrigerator. This was sheer curiosity and the intrigue of doing something forbidden. The morning had warmed up considerably; upon returning from school for lunch, I polished off the remaining six ounces of beer and disposed of the bottle. I don't recall any signs of inebriation during afternoon classes, just the refreshing taste of a cool brew.

After school, Roger and I, with several neighborhood kids, were playing in the expansive yard just south of the Waterbury's house, where Charlie and Grace, an elderly couple, had lived for decades. I was unaware that Dad upon arriving home had noticed that one of his Pabst Blue Ribbons was missing. To this day, I have no idea who "squealed:" Roger was with me, and Alan was too young to grasp the significance of my misdeed, so I thought. Anyway, Dad was an even tempered man very light on discipline. I don't recall ever receiving a spanking from him—except on this occasion.

I spotted Dad coming across Waterbury's backyard at a pace I hadn't seen before, heading straight for me. The synapses in my brain registered immediately, and adrenalin quickly flowed to my psychomotor system. This was a raw "fright and flight" response. I had never seen that look in his eyes before but knew it was meant for me.

I began to circle the field, as Dad attempted to close in. Around we went. When he felt that I was cornered, I reversed direction circling and taking the diagonal to avoid his rush. Dad was 38-years-old when I was born and this was 1948 putting him at age 47. He was trim and agile, but I was developing speed, cunning, and illusiveness. Friends stood on the sidelines enjoying the spectacle. Roger, no doubt, headed home to tell mother of events unfolding on the field. By this time, older brother Don had joined the hunt with Dad, and the two collaborated to trap the kid. One more move and, perhaps, I could escape, but where was I to go. Eventually, the chase would be over and my destiny a foregone conclusion. So, I made a heroic decision, heading straight for Dad and between his legs only to be snagged by Don on the other side.

The subsequent thrashing was minimal, and I suspect all had a good laugh at the sight of a grown man and teenager taking several exhausting minutes to capture the wily kid. This event left me neither traumatized nor resulted in my being a nascent alcoholic. Mom's primary concern was that my teacher would detect beer on my breath, report it to the principal, and our family would "make the evening news." Only embarrassment went through her mind, and nothing about the wayward path her middle son might be taking.

The Waterbury tract was the site of many football contests on fall afternoons. Dad had constructed a shower in our basement, much like a locker room, so that Roger and I could head straight to the cellar after a mud-soaked game. Our uniforms and equipment resulted from the charity of Coach Baxter who would pass along outdated helmets, shoulder pads, and jerseys to Roger and me. Department and sporting goods stores didn't carry such gear for youngsters in those days or, at least, not in Elkhorn and nearby towns. Anyway, there was no discretionary money for extravagance.

A favorite of our classic football matches was a "one-on-one" challenge with each brother taking turns kicking off or punting the ball to the other. While the kick returner ran to elude his adversary, the kicker attempted to nail the runner in his tracks. Our kick returning, pass receiving, tackling, and running skills were nurtured on that 35 x 20-yard turf that went by the name of Waterbury Field in our youth.

On a beautiful fall afternoon, several neighborhood boys, including our older brother, gathered at Waterbury for a spirited football contest. By age 16, Don was too big for the field, but he rifled a pass anyway on a "down and up" pattern directly toward the Waterbury's house. As I came up short attempting to haul in the errant pigskin, it spiraled through the first-floor window. We knew Mrs. Waterbury was home and could sense her stirring inside with glass scattered on the living room floor. My assignment on these occasions was to track down Roger and prevent him from racing home to tell mother of any misadventure. As I gathered myself and looked for my younger brother, all I could see was his backside high-tailing to our house, much as Allen Schoonover would witness at Camp Randall Stadium eight years later.

Don promptly detached the window frame and measured the opening. We cleaned up the broken pieces and headed on foot to the Elkhorn Hardware Store for a pane of glass. Soon, we returned, and as Don was inserting the new window, the frame slipped from its mooring and crashed to the ground. Back to the hardware store we went for another pane. Soon, the window was successfully installed, and, as we looked up, there stood Mrs. Waterbury observing it all.

The only remarks we heard of this event or any from that gentle couple were how respectful and considerate the Van boys always had been to them. What wonderful neighbors to put up with our energy, play, and noise over the years and never complain. Charlie Waterbury had an honorable career at the *Elkhorn Independent* as shop foreman. The Waterbury's had one child, an adopted daughter Elsie, who was affable and gracious. We only knew Elsie as an adult, who occasionally would bring home a boy friend that didn't seem to deserve her company.

♪

We humans run because by nature we are physical, energetic, playful creatures. For 99 percent of human history, people were "hunters and gatherers," dependent upon their physical and intuitive capabilities for survival. The past couple thousand years of civilization have not erased millions of years of evolutionary adaptation.

Children and adolescents express an energetic, athletic, and biological nature. As guardians of society, adults work to culturally suppress these traits—with some success by age 18. Adults, however, constantly are tempted by urges to be playful.

Stadiums, gymnasiums, tracks, and ball fields are modern arenas where participants, mostly the young, can "let off steam." It's been said, and I think accurately, that without football, as violent as it can be, society would have more wars. Adults, for the most part, are spectators. Inherently frustrated with such inactivity, many become obnoxious and unruly, belligerent and violent, not to mention overweight and out-of-shape. The physically active and attractive among us are poor spectators. Runners are prime examples of those who rebel at sitting and watching. They have been unleashed and exult in their physical freedom.

A consistent theme throughout modern intellectual history is the human need for play. The Greeks spoke continually of training the body, and the need for harmony between mind and body. Movement, thought, and creativity have been closely associated throughout history. Philosophers, writers, and others have sharpened their working days with extended walks. Henry David Thoreau once remarked, "I need every stride I take.... The length of my walking is the length of my writing."

In graduate school at the University of Colorado, I had a professor who took time each noon to run and workout. This was the pre-running boom era, and a sedentary classmate asked how he could afford the time daily away from teaching, research, and writing. The professor's reply was succinct: "I can't afford not to take the time to workout," he answered.

My running had purpose when I trained for races, but for the most part it was playful, athletic, and reflective. George Sheehan wrote, "I find my mind opens up when I run. All my ideas jell. I begin to see the theme of what I want to write." A few years ago, my running days diminished and bicycling became a substitute. In late October 2008, I underwent total hip replacement, and no longer run. As with exchanging the baton in a relay race, I made the transition from one form of movement (running) to another (bicycling) as smoothly as taking the baton from Billy Riese.

The thesis and content of this chapter took shape during a 60-minute bicycle ride this week.

About the Author

Richard Van Scotter is an author and citizen with degrees in economics and educational policy. He writes and speaks on educational issues, the political economy, and American culture. He is a regular contributor to journals and newspapers on cultural topics and social issues.

Index